STUDY GUIDE

CHRISTINA HARNETT
*The College of Notre Dame
of Maryland*

ABNORMAL
PSYCHOLOGY

THE PROBLEM
OF MALADAPTIVE BEHAVIOR

EIGHTH EDITION

IRWIN G. SARASON

BARBARA R. SARASON

PRENTICE HALL, *Upper Saddle River, New Jersey 07458*

© 1996 by PRENTICE-HALL, INC.
Simon and Schuster/A Viacom Company
Upper Saddle River, New Jersey 07458

10 9 8 7 6 5 4 3 2 1

ISBN 0-13-376476-1
Printed in the United States of America

TABLE OF CONTENTS

PREFACE

Your instructor has selected an excellent text for your introduction to the field of abnormal psychology. Sarason and Sarason's ABNORMAL PSYCHOLOGY: THE PROBLEM OF MALADAPTIVE BEHAVIOR (8th Edition), presents you with an up-to-date, comprehensive overview of the major forms of maladaptive behavior, including their symptoms, theories and treatments, found in this country today.

As you approach your study of this text, you will note that each chapter is organized in the following manner. The chapter begins with an outline of material to be presented and this serves as the "big picture" for a specific topic area. Each chapter will also include key terms that are important for you to know, diagnostic criteria for syndromes, and theoretical and research perspectives. Additionally, you will find that every chapter includes informative and interesting case vignettes in the form of "First Person Stories" and related information in boxes and tables. This information is especially important in helping you understand and apply material that you have learned. A special effort has been made by your authors in this area and you will find that the inclusion of this material truly makes the area of clinical psychology come to life.

This *Study Guide* is designed to maximize and reinforce your learning of text material, and to test your comprehension of it. To this end, each chapter contains the same format and elements. Each chapter begins with a CHAPTER OUTLINE that is identical to the one in your text. The KEY TERMS AND CONCEPTS section highlights technical terms and concepts that are pertinent to the field, and this material is drawn from the bold-faced terms found in every chapter. The CRITICAL THINKING QUESTIONS afford you an opportunity to integrate information, while the MULTIPLE CHOICE QUESTIONS assist you in identifying strengths and weaknesses in particular areas. The TRUE/FALSE and MATCHING items allow you to assess your recall and understanding of particular points made in the text. Lastly, you will find an ANSWER KEY located at the end of each work chapter.

Each instructor has his/her own biases in selecting material and formats for exams. Consequently, you may find some slight variance between the *Study Guide* and class exams. By working with your *Study Guide*, you should have a fairly realistic appraisal of your comprehension of text material and areas that may need further clarification by your instructor.

One last point deserves mention. Although great care has been taken to ensure that material in this *Study Guide* is accurate, mistakes can and do happen. Should you find a mistake (and we hope you don't), please bring it to the attention of your instructor and congratulate yourself. It means you are using your *Study Guide* correctly.

Welcome.

Chapter 1
ABNORMAL PSYCHOLOGY

CHAPTER OVERVIEW

This chapter introduces you to abnormal psychology and the concept of abnormal behavior. Abnormal behaviors are viewed as maladaptive behaviors, which are a function of three factors: situation-related stress, personal vulnerability, and coping-skill deficits. The epidemiology of maladaptive behavior is discussed and treatment facilities and treating professionals are described. Research techniques, methods of data analysis, and ethical concerns are reviewed.

CHAPTER OUTLINE

What Is Abnormal Behavior?
      The Stigma of Abnormal Behavior
      Adaptive and Maladaptive Behavior
      Vulnerability, Resiliency, and Coping

The Epidemiology of Maladaptive Behavior
      Prevalence, Incidence, and Risk Factors

Seeking Help for Abnormal Behavior
      Reasons for Clinical Contacts
      Sources of Help

Research in Abnormal Behavior
      Observing Behavior
      The Role of Theory
      The Research Journey
      Types of Research
      Research Design, Statistical Analyses, and Inference
      Ethical Aspects of Research

LEARNING OBJECTIVES

You should know:

1. that abnormal psychology focuses on the causes, consequences, and treatment of maladaptive behavior.

2. some of the beliefs of the general public that result in abnormal behavior being stigmatized.

3. the differences between adaptation and adjustment, and between maladaptive and deviant behavior.

4. the relationships between stress, coping, and vulnerability.

5. the main reasons why people seek clinical attention.

6. what epidemiological research is and how it is used.

7. the differences among clinical psychologists, psychiatrists, psychiatric social workers, and psychiatric nurses in training and in the kinds of work that they do.

8. the steps in the research journey, including the roles of independent and dependent variables, hypotheses, and descriptive and inferential statistics.

9. the strengths and weaknesses of the case study, correlational, longitudinal, and cross-sectional research methods.

10. the types and characteristics of experimental studies, including hypothesis-testing and behavior change experiments.

11. the ethical principles governing research, especially confidentiality, use of deception, informed consent, and research with those unable to give consent.

KEY TERMS AND CONCEPTS

Following is a list of key terms and concepts that are featured in the chapter and are important for you to know. Write out the definitions of each of these terms and check your answers with the definitions in the text.

abnormal psychology
adaptation
adjustment
maladaptive
resiliency
coping
coping skills
vulnerability
epidemiological research
prevalence
lifetime prevalence
incidence
risk factor
deinstitutionalize
clinical psychologist
psychiatrist
somatic therapies
psychiatric social worker
psychiatric nurse
counseling psychologist
self-observations
independent variables
dependent variables
hypothesis
descriptive statistics
inferential statistics
case study
correlational study
assessment study
longitudinal study
follow-up study
cross-sectional study
experiment
hypothesis testing experiment
behavior-change experiment
clinical trial
placebo
double blind

internal validity
external validity
measures of central tendency
mean
median
mode
measures of variability
range
standard deviation
null hypothesis
correlation coefficient
confounding
reactivity
demand characteristics
expectancy effects
sampling

CRITICAL THINKING QUESTIONS

In developing answers for the following questions, turn to the section of your chapter that covers the pertinent material. Read the section thoroughly before attempting to frame your answer.

1. How does the stigma of abnormal behavior impact the victim and society's reaction to the victim? In the public's perception, what causes abnormal behavior?

2. What is the meaning of "adaptation" and how does it differ from "adjustment"?

3. Deviant behavior is not always maladaptive. Explain. What factors are implied in the label "maladaptive"?

4. Define: stress, coping, and vulnerability. How are these terms related?

5. List the goals of epidemiological research. Define prevalence and incidence. What are risk factors and what is their value to a researcher?

6. What are the reasons people have for seeking help?

7. List the various types of mental health professionals presented in this chapter and identify their differences in terms of training and function.

8. Outline the important steps in conducting research. What is a theory and what function does it serve?

9. Describe the strengths and weaknesses of the following types of research strategies: case, correlational, longitudinal, and cross-sectional studies.

10. Experimental studies enable researchers to examine cause and effect relationships. How is this accomplished? List the types of experiments presented.

11. Discuss the differences between inferential and descriptive statistics. Explain the roles of measures of central tendency, measures of variability and the correlation coefficient in research.

12. What factors may undermine the validity of research results?

13. What are the ethical standards for conducting research?

MULTIPLE CHOICE

The following multiple choice questions will test your comprehension of the material presented in the chapter. Circle the correct choice for each question in the section, then compare your answers with those at the end of the chapter.

1. The term _____ refers to survival of the species.

    a. adjustment
    b. coping
    c. adaptation
    d. vulnerability

2. Which of the following statements is(are) true?

    a. All maladaptive behavior is deviant behavior.
    b. Deviant behavior is always maladaptive.
    c. There are few causes of maladaptive behavior.
    d. a & b.

3. How people react to situations that pose demands, constraints, or opportunities is called

    a. adaptation.
    b. coping.
    c. stress.
    d. vulnerability.

4.   Vulnerability is best defined as

       a. the likelihood of maladaptive responses in certain situations.
       b. the likelihood of maladaptive responses in all situations.
       c. the likelihood of the person being resilient in certain situations.
       d. the likelihood of the person being resilient in all situations.

5.   _____ refers to how people deal with difficulties and attempt to overcome them.

       a. Adaptation
       b. Adjustment
       c. Deviance
       d. Coping

6.   Clinical interventions are ways of helping people cope with _____ more effectively.

       a. adaptation
       b. coping
       c. stress
       d. vulnerability

7.   The rate of admissions to outpatient mental health services for the 18- to 24 year-old population is about

       a. 150 per 100,000.
       b. 1,100 per 100,000.
       c. 1,500 per 100,000.
       d. 2,500 per 100,000.

8.   The rate of the number of new cases during a defined period of time is called _____, while the rate of both new and old cases for a specific period is termed

       a. incidence; prevalence.
       b. prevalence; incidence.
       c. epidemiology; incidence.
       d. deviance; prevalence.

9.   Which of the following has been identified as a risk factor for violent behavior?

       a. being raised in a single parent home
       b. prior history of psychiatric hospitalization
       c. habitual alcohol use and dependence
       d. low motivation or drive

10. According to Swanson and others (1990),

   a. there is no relationship between the rate of reported violent behaviors and the number of diagnostic symptoms assigned to a person by a clinician.
   b. the greater the number of clinical symptoms present, the greater the likelihood that violence will be among them.
   c. violent people often possess no other clinical symptoms.
   d. the older the individual, the more clinical symptoms one observes.

11. Which of the following is not a risk factor associated with increased rates for mental disorders?

   a. marital happiness
   b. contact with friends
   c. low self-esteem
   d. education

12. Mary and John have been married for seven years. Recently, John confessed to an affair because guilt kept him from sleeping. If John seeks help from a clinician it is most probably because of

   a. his age.
   b. his unhappiness.
   c. the fact adultery is a crime.
   d. the nature of his admission.

13. Select the following statement that is true.

   a. Since the 1960's, deinstitutionalization has been on the decrease.
   b. Community-based care is delivered in several forms including group homes.
   c. The failure of states to mandate community-based treatment has resulted in an increase in the number of inpatient treatment facilities.
   d. Community-based treatment is less effective overall than inpatient treatment.

14. A _____ has a medical degree and is allowed to prescribe medication.

   a. clinical psychologist
   b. psychiatrist
   c. psychiatric social worker
   d. psychotherapist

15. Because of different theoretical orientations, psychologists tend to
emphasize _____, while psychiatrists focus on _____.

   a. diagnosis; medication regimens.
   b. the importance between onset and course of a mental illness;
   factors related to onset of the illness.
   c. the relationship between a person's psychological state of mind and relationships
   with friends and family; a biological approach to treatment.
   d. somatic therapies; specific forms of talk therapy.

16. Which of the following would likely be the first steps in the research process?

   a. observing and describing behaviors
   b. hypothesis formation and developing operational definitions
   c. interpretation of data and theory formation
   d. hospital and clinical situation application

17. A clinician observes that whenever a particular staff member comes in contact
with patient X, the patient displays aggressive behavior. Which type of observation
is the clinician using?

   a. consequences of behavior
   b. stimuli that elicit particular types of responses
   c. behavioral response to the stimuli
   d. subjective responses to the stimuli

18. A useful theory should be

   a. testable.
   b. correct.
   c. intuitive.
   d. controversial.

19. In a study testing the effects of listening to music on anxiety, the music would be the
_____, while anxiety would be the _____.

   a. independent variable; dependent variable.
   b. dependent variable; independent variable.
   c. hypothesis; dependent variable.
   d. correlational evidence; dependent variable.

20. A(n)_____ involves the in-depth study of an individual's behavior.

   a. case study
   b. correlational study

c. assessment study
d. self-observation

21. Correlational studies allow the researcher

   d

   a. to follow up patients by retesting them.
   b. to study a single individual over a long period of time
   c. to determine that variable A caused variable B.
   d. to establish relationships between variables.

22. Observing the same group of subjects for a long period of time is typical of

   b

   a. a survey.
   b. a longitudinal study.
   c. a cross-sectional study.
   d. a self-observation.

23. Which of the following is not a problem when doing longitudinal studies?

   d

   a. They tend to take a long time to complete.
   b. They are often expensive.
   c. Subjects used in the study may move or die.
   d. They are used much too often to be of real value.

24. In one study, subjects were given a self-report measure of anxiety. Six months later, these same individuals took the test again to see if their level of anxiety had changed. This study was probably designed to be a _____ study.

   d

   a. hypothetical
   b. longitudinal
   c. cross-sectional
   d. follow-up

25. A researcher wants to find out the average height and weight of children between the ages of two and five years. The most efficient way of gathering this information would be to do a(n)

   b

   a. longitudinal study.
   b. cross-sectional study.
   c. prevalence measure.
   d. inferential design.

26. Hypothesis-testing experiments

   b

   a. tend to pose many ethical problems for researchers.
   b. involve making a prediction based on a theory.
   c. are always double-blind.
   d. involve the development of new therapeutic techniques.

27. A researcher wants to test the effectiveness of a new drug for depression. She obtains two comparable groups of depressed patients. To the one group, she administers the new drug; while the other group receives some form of control treatment. This methodology may be described as

   b

   a. a double-blind.
   b. a clinical trial.
   c. an assessment procedure.
   d. a follow-up study.

28. Harlow's research with monkeys suggested that

   d

   a. amphetamines caused response stereotypy.
   b. stimulant medication had a calming effect.
   c. stimulant drugs made monkeys less responsive to reinforcement.
   d. early separation from mother produced negative effects.

29. In a double-blind study, neither the subjects not the experimenter are aware

   c

   a. that an experiment is being conducted.
   b. that a placebo will be used.
   c. what the independent variable will be.
   d. of what dependent variable might occur.

30. Internal validity refers to _____, while external validity refers to_____.

   a

   a. experimental conditions; generalization of findings to the real world.
   b. the soundness of the hypothesis; the ability of the hypothesis to predict behavior outside the laboratory.
   c. manipulation of the dependent variable; manipulation of the independent variable.
   d. none of the above.

31. A study finds that the average age for first drink of an alcoholic beverage among teenagers is 3.4 years of age. This statistic is a

   b

   a. median
   b. mean
   c. mode
   d. correlation

32.   Which of the following refers to changes in behavior that occur when subjects are aware of the fact that they are being observed?

    a. confounding
    b. expectancy effects
    c. reactivity
    d. demand characteristics

33.   If valid conclusions are to be drawn from a study, then

    a. the population should not be representative of the sample.
    b. the researcher should be blind to the sample under study.
    c. confounding must be maximized.
    d. the sampling must be representative of the population.

TRUE/FALSE QUESTIONS

Indicate whether each statement is true or false. Check your answers at the end of this chapter.

1. F   Adaptation refers to individual mastery of the environment.

2. T   Heredity can increase vulnerability.

3. T   Some areas of the U.S. have higher rates for schizophrenia than other areas.

4. F   The occurrence of a given condition at a particular point in time is called prevalence.

5. T   Less educated people have higher rates of diagnosed mental disorders than people who have more education.

6. F   In the past ten years there has been an increase in the number of beds in state mental hospitals.

7. F   Psychologists prescribe medications for their clients.

8. F   The last step in the research process is to analyze the results.

9. T   For the most part, explanations of behavior occur after the fact in case studies.

10. F   One limitation of the assessment study is that it provides little if any useful information.

11. T Experiments on animals have been conducted to investigate both biological and social factors in behavior.

12. F Placebos are inactive substances that never affect a person's behavior.

13. F Descriptive statistics allow the researcher to test comparisons between groups.

14. T The null hypothesis states that there is no difference between two groups.

15. F Occasionally, prisoners or mental patients must be forced to participate in research for their own good.

MATCHING

Match the following terms with information provided below. The answers may be found at the end of this chapter.

a. confounding
b. demand characteristics
c. risk factor
d. deinstitutionalize
e. somatic therapies
f. inferential statistics

g. mode
h. social worker
i. hypothesis
j. placebo
k. independent variable

_g_ most frequently occurring score among subjects
_i_ an educated guess
_h_ focuses on link between disordered behavior and home environment
_k_ manipulated by researcher to assess impact on outcome measure
_f_ allows the null hypothesis to be tested
_a_ results from failure to control other influences on the dependent variable
_j_ an inactive substance
_d_ release from a psychiatric hospital
_c_ identified on basis of a relationship between two variables
_e_ includes use of drugs and electroconvulsive therapy
_b_ subject's perception of what is expected of him/her

ANSWER KEY

Multiple Choice

1. c
2. a
3. c
4. a
5. d
6. d
7. b
8. a
9. c
10. b
11. c
12. b
13. b
14. b
15. c
16. a
17. c

18. a
19. a
20. a
21. d
22. b
23. d
24. d
25. b
26. b
27. b
28. d
29. c
30. a
31. b
32. c
33. d

True/False

1. T
2. T
3. T
4. T
5. T
6. F
7. F
8. F

9. T
10. F
11. T
12. F
13. F
14. T
15. F

Matching

g
i
h
k
f
a
j
d
c
e
b

Chapter 2
THE HISTORICAL BACKGROUND OF ABNORMAL PSYCHOLOGY

CHAPTER OVERVIEW

The focus of this chapter is on the historical context of the causes and treatment of abnormal behavior from ancient times to present. Recurring themes as to the causes and treatment for mental illness will be presented and notable individuals and movements highlighted. The chapter closes with a discussion of the organic versus psychological perspectives on the causality of abnormal behavior.

CHAPTER OUTLINE

Historical Views of Abnormal Behavior
        The Ancient Western World
        The Middle Ages
        The Renaissance
        The Age of Reason and the Enlightenment
        The Reform Movement

Psychological and Organic Views of Abnormal Behavior
        The Psychological Approach
        The Organic Approach
        The Approaches Converge

The Stage Is Set

LEARNING OBJECTIVES

You should know:

1.   the three main recurring theories about the cause of maladaptive behavior.

2.   what the practices of shamanism and trephining are and how they relate to early concepts of abnormal behavior.

3.   the ideas and approaches to treatment of deviant behavior of the ancient Greeks, Hippocrates, Socrates, Plato, and Aristotle, and of the Roman physician Galen.

4. the general approaches to deviance during the Middle Ages; the contributions of St. Augustine, Paracelsus, and Huarte.

5. the increasingly rational approach to abnormal behavior in the Renaissance and the efforts made by Johann Weyer to this development.

6. that the 17th and 18th centuries saw the end of superstition and a commitment to rationality, scientific method, and humane treatment of the mentally ill. The ideas of Spinoza, Gall, Cullen, and Mesmer should be understood.

7. the major events of the Reform Movement in Europe, including the work of Pinel and Pussin in France, the 1815 "Parliamentarian Inquiry" in England, and the growth of treatment for children.

8. the shape that the Reform movement took in America, reflected in the work of Benjamin Rush, Dorothea Dix, and Clifford Beers.

9. the psychological and organic approaches and how they merged.

10. how current ideas about deviant behavior have historical as well as cultural roots.

KEY TERMS AND CONCEPTS

Following is a list of key terms and concepts that are featured in the chapter and are important for you to know. Write out the definitions of each of these terms and check your answers with the definition in the text.

exorcism
shaman
trephination
organismic point of view
humors
natural fool
non compos mentis
physiognomy
phrenology
moral treatment
rational thinking
irrational thought
hysterics

CRITICAL THINKING QUESTIONS

In developing answers for the following questions, turn to that section of your chapter that covers the pertinent material. Read the section thoroughly before attempting to frame your answer.

1. What are the commonly recurring themes in history of the causes of abnormal behavior? - Supernatural / Magical forces - Medical - Psychological

2. What was the practice of trephining and what therapeutic value was it supposed to have? a sharp tool (stone) used to make a hole in the skull - 2 centimeters - to permit demonic spirits to escape. in diameter

3. How did the ancient Greeks conceptualize organic and psychological factors as causing abnormal behavior? Homer - a punishment for offenses against the gods. Hippocrates - looked to brain to explain why people behave as they do (epileptic seizures - brain disease). Socrates - self exploration + reasoning - using inquiry to further knowledge

(left margin note for 3/4) Plato - disturbed behavior grew out of conflicts but emotion + reasoning - Aristotle - believed in body needed to be in balance for reasoning to prevail.

4. In what way did the treatment of abnormal behavior change during the Middle Ages? Describe the contributions of St. Augustine and Paracelsus. laid ground work for modern psychodynamic theory (used introspection to discuss the mental process). Mental process - invasion by Barbarian tribes + growth of Christian religion (causing social unrest) (comforted people). maladaptation caused by natural phenomena (astrology) - (fear + terror) Christian spirit of charity.

5. The Renaissance was a period of "enlightened humanism." Explain this term and its impact on the treatment of mental illness. Period of increased humanism curiosity about nature, & interest in scholarship (Johann Weyer - psychological conflict + disturbed interpersonal relationships cause mental disorder) Enlightened humanism - saved countless lives. Need to treat disturbed people medically rather than theologically.

6. Describe how science and rationalism replaced spiritual conceptualizations of abnormal behaviors. Age of Reason + Enlightenment (1600's - 1700's) Scientific Method for understanding the natural world. Major advances in astronomy, biology, & chemistry. Spinoza - argued the the mind + body are inseparable. Psychological process, although not observable, are equally important to mental processes of natural world.

7. Who was Anton Mesmer and what was his "therapeutic approach"? What concept of his is still utilized in treatment today? A Viennese physician - idea of animal magnetism. All people were endowed w/ a special magnetic fluid (a kind of sixth sense) that when liberated could cure & prevent all illnesses. He believed he possessed an unusual abundance of the fluid + could treat it (remove) gesture w/ hands + movement - a magnetic force

(left margin note for 8) business man Beers - A Mind That Found Itself (Founder of personal experiences (American Psychiatry) informed citizens reform group - now the National Committee for Mental Hygiene (Health) promoted social programs.

8. Pinel, Rush, Dix, and Beers held views that directly impacted the treatment of institutionalized individuals. What were these views and how did they bring about reform? Pinel believed deranged required humane care + treatment (Russia). former patient (of chains - treatment - bleeding, purging + water cures) Rush - believed madness was caused by engorgement of the blood vessels of the brain. Dix - school teacher devoted to reform. Visited penitentiaries, jails, etc. where mentally ill were kept. Results → 32 mental hospitals constructed.

9. Describe the issues involved in the controversy between organic and psychological explanations of abnormal behavior.

10. In 1992, Salem, Massachusetts celebrated its 300th anniversary of the original "witch trials." It is now commonly held that this movement was fostered by mass hysteria. Explain how you think this might have happened.

(bottom handwritten notes)
#9 Psychological - German Heinroth - mental illness resulted from internal conflicts bet. unacceptable impulses + the guilt generated by those illnesses. (similar to Freud)
Organic - Griesinger - most mental disorders caused by the direct or indirect influence of disturbances of the brain. "Mental Diseases are Brain Diseases"
Emil Kraepelin - attempted to construct a classification system that would encompass most of the disorders that required treatment + hospitalization.
Converge - Charcot - believed organic disturbances were important but also psychological approach

MULTIPLE CHOICE

The following multiple choice questions will test your comprehension of the material presented in the chapter. Circle the correct choice for each question in the section, then compare your answers with those at the end of the chapter.

1. By examining the historical background of abnormal behavior, one can

   a. see how there are recurring theories of why people develop psychological problems.
   b. see that we have been able to discard the old, obsolete methods for treating psychological problems.
   c. become aware that much of what seems modern only developed after science proved how incorrect past views were.
   d. see how there was no attempt to treat troubled people in ancient times.

2. Trephination involves

   a. having the shaman remove a "demon possessed" stone from the victim's ear or mouth.
   b. making a small hole in the skull.
   c. a generally fatal procedure carried out in a non-sterile environment.
   d. casting out evil spirits through prayer.

3. _____ proposed the "organismic point of view", which sees behavior as a product of the totality of psychological processes.

   a. Hippocrates
   b. Plato
   c. Socrates
   d. Aristotle

4. According to Galen, _____ were believed to be related to the temperamental qualities of an individual.

   a. brain dysfunctions
   b. demons
   c. irrational thoughts
   d. humors

5.   Saint Augustine helped lay the groundwork for modern

      a. humanistic psychology.
      b. behavioral theories.
      c. organic views of mental disorders.
      d. psychodynamic theory.

6.   The *Malleus Maleficarum* was a

      a. book describing correct techniques for trephination.
      b. book of spells supposedly used by witches.
      c. reference book used by church authorities to identify witches.
      d. book written by St. Augustine about psychological problems.

7.   Spinosa believed that

      a. mind and body were separate entities.
      b. mind and body were inseparable.
      c. exorcism was the only effective way to eliminate demonic possession.
      d. St. Augustine was incorrect in his assumptions about human behavior.

8.   A person during the nineteenth century might visit Franz Gall, who would attempt
      to identify personality characteristics by feeling the bumps on the person's skull. The
      technique Gall used was called

      a. phrenology.
      b. bacquet.
      c. mesmerism.
      d. animal magnetism.

9.   The Scottish physician, Cullen, treated his patients with

      a. bloodletting and physiotherapy.
      b. music and food.
      c. relaxation and baths.
      d. prayers and fasting.

10.   Anton Mesmer believed that people developed psychological problems because

      a. they were possessed by demons.
      b. the bumps on the skull inaccurately reflected underlying personality structures.
      c. people ate poor diets.
      d. their magnetic fluids were out of balance.

11. Mesmer's treatment appears to have been effective because of the patient's

    a. physical health.
    b. belief in the gods.
    c. age.
    d. suggestibility.

12. The term "bedlam" derived from

    a. Pinel's "Treatise on Insanity."
    b. the work of William Cullen.
    c. the atmosphere at St. Mary of Bethlehem hospital.
    d. comments regarding Virginia's hospital for "ideots and lunatics."

13. The movement of reform in Europe led directly to

    a. children being placed in half-way houses.
    b. the creation of institutions for psychologically disturbed kids.
    c. the popularity of the psychoanalytic movement.
    d. the foster care movement.

14. The people most responsible for the reform movement in America were

    a. Pinel, Pussin, and Mesmer.
    b. Hone, Cruikshank, and Facquier.
    c. Rush, Dix, and Beers.
    d. Freud, Heinroth, and Griesinger.

15. Freud's theories about mental processes were greatly influenced by the nineteenth century belief that

    a. focused on irrational feelings and emotions as the basis for disturbed behavior.
    b. focused on rational thinking as the way to achieve personal and social adjustment.
    c. animal magnetism as an important force in psychological maladjustment.
    d. physical illnesses as the basic cause for all psychological problems.

16. Clifford Beer's book, *A Mind That Found Itself,*

    a. is directly responsible for the development of the insanity plea.
    b. argues in favor of the organic view of maladaptive behavior.
    c. was instrumental in gaining popular support for the mental health movement in America.
    d. led Freud to develop a theory of unconscious processes.

17. The organic approach assumes that

a. irrational feelings lead to physical illnesses.
b. animal magnetism eventually resulted in insanity.
c. most mental disorders have a physical basis.
d. most psychological problems are caused by deficiencies in rational thought processes.

18. Which of the following theorists held that dementia praecox and manic-depressive psychosis were due to specific organic causes?

a. Heinroth
b. Charcot
c. Mesmer
d. Kraeplin

19. The French neurologist Jean Charcot combined the organic and psychological approaches in that he

a. believed that organic disturbances were important but used a psychological approach in studying and treating them.
b. believed that psychological conflicts were at the root of mental disturbances but used drugs and medicines to treat them.
c. thought that if the irrational thoughts and conflicts were eliminated, organic health could be restored.
d. worked with Freud to develop the neurological approach to treating unconscious conflicts.

20. Charcot treated patients suffering from hysteria with

a. la belle indifference.
b. hypnosis.
c. the bacquet.
d. moral treatment.

21. Janet believed that hysteria was caused by

a. physical weaknesses caused by an imbalance in bodily fluids.
b. repressed wishes and conflicts, mainly of a sexual or hostile nature.
c. dreams that were upsetting to the conscious mind.
d. certain ideas splitting off from conscious experience.

22.   Originally, Sigmund Freud had received training

       a. as a neurologist.
       b. in mesmerism.
       c. as a specialist in the development and administration of moral treatment
       programs.
       d. as a physiognomist.

23.   Whether or not a behavior is considered deviant is based on

       a. scientific evaluation and careful observation.
       b. evidence that an organic problem is present.
       c. society's values and attitudes at the time the behavior occurs.
       d. whether there is evidence of hysteria in the behavior.

TRUE/FALSE QUESTIONS

Indicate whether each statement is true or false. Check your answers at the end of this chapter.

1.   The idea that abnormal behavior can be explained by supernatural or magical forces like evil spirits can still be encountered today.

2.   In ancient Greece, mental deviations came to be viewed as natural phenomena for which rational treatments might be developed.

3.   During the Middle Ages, music and dance were thought to cure insanity by restoring the chemical balance within the body.

4.   The term "non compos mentis" is Latin for mentally retarded from birth.

5.   During the seventeenth and eighteenth centuries, people accepted the idea that demons and supernatural forces were the causes of abnormal behaviors.

6.   Gall's theory that bumps on the skull reflect underlying brain structures is called physiognomy.

7.   Moral treatment involved exorcism and an attempt to improve the morals of people in insane asylums.

8.   Beer's book, A *Mind that Found Itself,* demonstrates that humane and humanistic treatment was widespread and popular during the early 1900's.

T 9. Johann Heinroth theorized that mental illness was the result of internal conflicts generated between unacceptable impulses and guilt.

T 10. According to Charcot, hysterics were people who suffered from organic symptoms for which no organic causes could be found.

T 11. Theories of abnormality are almost never brand new.

MATCHING

Match the following terms with information provided below. The answers may be found at the end of this chapter.

a. natural fool   f. hysteric
b. shaman   g. hypnotism
c. exorcism   h. black bile
d. physiognomy   i. Plato
e. irrational thought   j. St. Augustine

__h__ one of four humors
__f__ characterized by "la belle indifference"
__c__ removing evil through counter magic and prayer
__a__ mentally retarded person with child-like intellectual qualities
__d__ used to judge personality characteristics on the basis of physical appearance
__j__ wrote "Confessions" using introspection
__b__ medicine man who is a spiritual medium
__e__ 19th century explanation for normal and abnormal behavior
__g__ based on subject's suggestibility
__i__ believed the mentally ill should be placed in the care of relatives

ANSWER KEY

Multiple Choice

1. A	13. B
2. B	14. C
3. B	15. A
4. D	16. C
5. D	17. C
6. C	18. D
7. B	19. A
8. A	20. B
9. A	21. D
10. D	22. A
11. D	23. C
12. C	

True/False

1. T	7. F
2. T	8. F
3. T	9. T
4. F	10. T
5. F	11. T
6. F	

Matching

h
f
c
a
d
j
b
e
g
i

Chapter 3
THEORETICAL PERSPECTIVES ON MALADAPTIVE BEHAVIOR

CHAPTER OVERVIEW

The role of theory in the field of abnormal psychology is presented in this section. Several theories representing the biological, psychodynamic, behavioral, cognitive, humanistic-existential and community-cultural perspectives are featured and discussed. The chapter closes with a look at the integration of approaches to maladaptive behavior.

CHAPTER OUTLINE

The Role of Theory in Abnormal Psychology
> The Orientation of this Book

The Biological Perspective
> Biological Influences in Abnormal Behavior
> The Neurosciences Revolution
> Integration of Biological and Psychological Systems

The Psychodynamic Perspective
> Freud and Psychoanalysis
> Contemporary Approaches to Psychoanalysis
> Evaluating Psychoanalytic Theory

The Behavioral Perspective
> Classical Conditioning
> Operant Conditioning
> Social Learning Theory

The Cognitive Perspective
> Maladaptive Behavior and Cognition
> Cognitive Therapies

The Humanistic-Existential Perspective
> Rogers' Conception of the Self
> The Existential Point of View

The Community-Cultural Perspective
     Social Roles and Labeling
     Contributions of the Community-Cultural Perspective

An Integrative Approach

LEARNING OBJECTIVES

You should know:

1.   how theories of maladaptive behavior can be useful.

2.   what role genetic factors, the nervous system, and the endocrine glands play in influencing behavior.

3.   Freud's theory of psychosexual development, his view of the psychic apparatus, and how these relate to clinical psychoanalysis.

4.   the approach to psychoanalytic theory of the Neo-Freudians, Jung, Adler, and Erikson, and of the object relations theories and self-psychologists.

5.   the differences between classical and operant conditioning and how they are applied in therapeutic situations.

6.   how the social-learning and cognitive perspectives view the etiology of maladaptive behavior, and that the ideas of Bandura, Ellis, Kelly, and Beck are based on these perspectives.

7.   Rogers' conceptualization of optimal adjustment and the fully functioning person and the method of psychotherapy derived from his ideas.

8.   the existential ideas of authentic and inauthentic behavior and what the role of therapy is from this point of view.

9.   the community-cultural perspective on abnormal behavior, including social-causation and social selection theories and the ideas of Goffman on social roles.

10.   what the integrative approach is and its special value in conceptualizing human maladaptive behavior.

KEY TERMS AND CONCEPTS

Following is a list of key terms and concepts that are featured in the chapter and are important for you to know. Write out the definitions of each of these terms and check your answers with the definitions in the text.

biological perspective
psychodynamic perspective
behavioral perspective
cognitive perspective
humanistic-existential perspective
community-cultural perspective
body
mind
chromosome
chromosomal anomalies
genes
locus
karyotypes
genome
deoxyribonucleic acid
penetrance
population genetics
behavior genetics
behavior geneticist
monozygotic
dizygotic
concordance
central nervous system
peripheral nervous system
somatic system
autonomic system
neuron
axon
dendrites
neurotransmitter
synapse
cerebral cortex
electroencephalogram
limbic system
hypothalamus
endorphins
endocrines
stressor
adrenal cortex

corticotrophin-releasing factor
adrenocortico-trophic hormone
adrenal corticosteriod
neuroscience
substantia nigra
computed tomography
magnetic resonance imaging
magnetic resonance spectroscopy
single photon emission computed tomography
positron emission tomography
psychoneuroimmunology
antigens
lymphocytes
psychic determinism
conscious
preconscious
unconscious
libido
oral psychosexual stage
anal psychosexual stage
phallic psychosexual stage
genital psychosexual stage
fixation
regress
id
ego
superego
primary process thinking
pleasure principle
secondary process thinking
anxiety
defense mechanism
repression
psychoanalysis
free association
object relations theorists
splitting
self psychology
behavioral perspective
determinism
reinforcer
positive reinforcer
negative reinforcer
punishment
extinction

classical conditioning
conditioned stimulus
unconditioned response
unconditioned stimulus
conditioned response
escape responses
avoidance responses
systematic desensitization
operant conditioning
shaping
schedule
social learning theory
modeling
vicarious learning
social facilitation
copying
identification
role playing
implicit learning
cognitive perspective
schemata
self-efficacy
hypothetical constructs
intervening variables
personal constructs
rational-emotive therapy
fixed role therapy
self-actualization
authentically
inauthentically
social-causation theories
social-selection theory
social roles
labeling
mediators

CRITICAL THINKING QUESTIONS

In developing answers for the following questions, turn to that section of your chapter that covers the pertinent material. Read the section thoroughly before attempting to frame your answer.

1.   In what ways are theories of maladaptive behavior useful?

2. From the biological perspective, what are the physiological causes of abnormal behavior?

3. Define the following terms: genetic penetrance, behavior genetics, and genetic concordance.

4. Explain the nature versus nurture controversy. What is the position held by most psychologists?

5. Describe the new fields of neuroscience and psychoneuroimmunology.

6. What are the underlying assumptions regarding the causes of human behavior from the psychodynamic perspective?

7. Explain the function of defense mechanisms. List the defenses.

8. Outline the major ideas of the neo-Freudians.

9. Discuss how learning theorists view behavior. Define and give examples of positive and negative reinforcement, punishment and extinction.

10. Compare and contrast classical and operant conditioning.

11. Explain the role of modeling and covert mediators in the social learning explanations of abnormal behavior.

12. How do cognitive psychologists differ from those of the psychodynamic perspective in their study of the psychological processes involved in abnormal behavior?

13. How have learning theorists like Dollard and Miller, Kelly, and Bandura incorporated cognitions into their approaches of abnormal behavior?

14. Explain Ellis' view of maladaptive behavior. How does rational-emotive therapy attempt to deal with irrational beliefs?

15. How does Beck attempt to alter maladaptive cognitions during therapy?

16. Describe the humanistic-existential theories. In what ways do they differ from the behaviorist and psychodynamic perspective?

17. Briefly summarize the community-cultural perspective on abnormal behavior.

18. What is the difference between social-causation and social-selection?

19. Describe the interactive approach to the study of abnormal behavior.

MULTIPLE CHOICE

The following multiple choice questions will test your comprehension of the material presented in the chapter. Circle the correct choice for each item in the section, then compare your answers with those at the end of the chapter.

1.   The biological perspective

       a. became popular during the seventeenth century.
       b. gained popularity with the discovery of the link between bodily infections/defects and disordered behavior.
       c. suggests that high levels of psychological stress are responsible for psychological disorders.
       d. has established that there is a physiological cause for all psychological disorders.

b

2.   A major factor in some genetic abnormalities appears to be

       a. irregularities in the structure or number of an individual's chromosomes.
       b. the absence of DNA.
       c. the high rate of penetrance.
       d. none of the above

a

3.   Which of the following represents a correct association?

       a. monozygotic - chromosomal anomaly
       b. monozygotic - fraternal twins
       c. dizygotic - fraternal twins
       d. dizygotic - identical twins

c

4.   _____ in twin studies refers to the relationship between twins or other family members with respect to a given characteristic or trait.

       a. Penetrance
       b. Anomalies
       c. Psychoimmunology
       d. Concordance

d

5.   The fact that there is not a 100% concordance rate for schizophrenia between identical twins suggests

       a. error measurement in those studies.
       b. a genetic mutation.

c

c. the environment influences behavior.
d. that the twins are actually dizygotic.

6. Today, most psychologists view behavior to be a function of

a. nature only.
b. nurture only.
c. nature and nurture.
d. nurture if siblings, but nature if identical twins.

7. The central nervous system includes

a. the brain and spinal cord.
b. the glands and hormones which regulate behaviors.
c. the thymus and adrenal glands.
d. 100% of the nerve cells in the body.

8. A _____ is a messenger chemical sent to dendrite receptor sites.

a. synapse
b. axon
c. neuron
d. none of the above

9. In the brain, the _____ controls our distinctive human behavior, while the _____
    is responsible for hearing, vision, body sensations and other processes.

a. hypothalamus; cerebral cortex
b. cortex; cerebral cortex
c. cerebral cortex; cortex
d. cortex; hypothalamus

10. Endorphins are associated with

a. chromosomal anomalies.
b. opiate receptors in the brain reward system.
c. endocrine hormones.
d. EEG spikes characteristic of petit mal epilepsy.

11. Which of the following is (are) true?

a. The development of the brain is not influenced by environmental factors.
b. The brain uses the outside world to shape itself.
c. The brain goes through critical periods in which its cells require stimulation to
develop certain functions.
d. Both b and c.

12. Under stress, the hypothalamus releases a substance called

a. corticotrophin-releasing factor.
b. corticosteriod.
c. adrenocorticotrophic-releasing factor.
d. endorphin

13. A _____ would be a neuroscience specialist who might conduct an investigation on the relationship between Alzheimers disease and abnormalities in the brain structure.

a. neurochemist
b. neuropsychologist
c. neuroendocrinologist
d. neuropathologist

14. Select the following statement that is true.

a. It appears that many factors may cause mental illness.
b. Recent research confirms the fact that most mental illness is primarily due to brain abnormalities.
c. Deficiencies in the command center of the brain have not been found to be responsible for mental illness.
d. The stress of daily living, although worrisome, does not contribute to mental illness.

15. _____ is a form of brain imaging used to study subjects while they perform various kinds of cognitive tasks.

a. Computed tomography
b. Single photon emission computed tomography
c. Magnetic resonance imaging
d. Positron emission tomography

16. Which of the following is (are) true of sleep?

a. Bodily processes slow down at sleep onset.
b. Sleep disturbances are rare in the U. S. population.
c. Exercise probably deepens sleep.
d. Both a & c.

17. Psychoneuroimmunology involves the study of

   a. antigens and lymphocytes.
   b. psychoactive drug actions on psychotic behavior.
   c. psychological, neural, and immunological processes.
   d. the pain-relieving properties of endorphins.

18. The two major tasks of the immune system are

   a. reproduction and distribution of antigens.
   b. producing and dispersing endorphins.
   c. producing ACTH and deactivation of the hypothalamus.
   d. recognition and removal/inactivation of foreign materials.

19. Research on the relationship between bereavement and the immune system

   a. has shown little promise in light of new discoveries in the neurosciences.
   b. indicates that there appears to be a relationship between these variables.
   c. demonstrates that the absence of a social support network for the bereaved exacerbates suppression of the immune system.
   d. both b & c.

20. The psychodynamic perspective is based on the idea that

   a. stress can trigger psychological problems.
   b. stress can trigger physical disorders.
   c. thoughts and emotions are important causes of behaviors.
   d. psychological disorders are caused by hormonal imbalances.

21. Which of the following is the correct order for Freud's psychosexual stages of development?

   a. oral, anal, phallic, latency, genital
   b. oral, anal, latency, phallic, genital
   c. anal oral, phallic, latency, genital
   d. latency, oral, anal, phallic, genital

22. Which of the following statements is accurate regarding the functioning of the psychic apparatus according to Freud?

   a. The ego uses guilt to keep the id in line.
   b. Primary process thinking is found in children but not in adults.
   c. The ego is the only structure present in the infant.
   d. The id is concerned with the maximization of pleasure.

23. The most basic defense mechanism is

   _c_

   a. displacement.
   b. denial.
   c. repression.
   d. sublimation.

24. _____ involves expressing an unacceptable impulse by transforming it into its opposite.

   _b_

   a. Projection
   b. Reaction formation
   c. Regression
   d. Sublimation

25. Freud would view a 10-year-old child who begins bed wetting after a new sibling is born as utilizing the defense mechanism of

   _b_

   a. sublimation
   b. regression
   c. reaction formation
   d. projection

26. _____ viewed development as a life-long process proceeding in stages.

   _b_

   a. Kelly
   b. Erikson
   c. Alder
   d. Freud

27. _____ believed that psychological disorders were the direct result of deficits in the structure of the self.

   _d_
   Kohut

   a. Freud
   b. Adler
   c. Bandura
   d. None of the above

28. You have a headache and take an aspirin. The headache goes away. Your behavior of aspirin-taking has been

   _b_

   a. extinguished.
   b. negatively reinforced.
   c. punished.
   d. positively reinforced.

29. Which of the following mechanisms of behavior change results in a decrease in the frequency of the behavior?

    a. positive reinforcement
    b. negative reinforcement
    c. shaping
    d. extinction

30. Systematic desensitization procedures rely most heavily upon

    a. classical conditioning principles.
    b. operant conditioning principles.
    c. punishment.
    d. negative reinforcement principles.

31. Answering a telephone has been

    a. operantly conditioned.
    b. classically conditioned.
    c. extinguished through shaping.
    d. both b & c.

32. Bandura proposed that

    a. all behaviors were learned through reinforcement.
    b. modeling is ineffective as a learning tool.
    c. no individual learns vicariously.
    d. a behavior can be learned without reinforcement.

33. Self-efficacy refers to

    a. irrational beliefs.
    b. hypothetical constructs.
    c. convictions about personal effectiveness.
    d. the mental life of the individual and personal schemata.

34. Rational-Emotive therapy is based on the idea that

    a. disturbed emotions result in abnormal behaviors.
    b. anxiety and guilt decrease feelings of self-efficacy.
    c. people are motivated to strive toward self-actualization.
    d. irrational thoughts cause emotional overreactions.

35. Beck's concept of schema refers to

c

    a. a person's plan for achieving self-actualization.
    b. experiences in later life that affect our ability to deal with trauma.
    c. a cognitive structure in a particular domain.
    d. an individual's cognitive structure that serves as a conscience.

36. A therapist asks her client to act out a new role that has been the focus of treatment. Most probably, this therapist's orientation has been influenced by

b

    a. Beck.
    b. Kelly.
    c. Perls.
    d. Ellis

37. Humanistic-existential theorists believe that

c

    a. psychology should focus on observable behaviors.
    b. psychological problems are a product of illogical thoughts.
    c. inner experiences and a search for the meaning of existence should be the focus of psychology.
    d. the job of the therapist is to help clients restructure their thinking and replace maladaptive thoughts.

38. Which of the following represents a similarity between the ideas of Freud and the perspective of Rogers?

b

    a. Both believed the roots of anxiety lie in unconscious impulses.
    b. Both developed their theories from the observations of clients in psychotherapy.
    c. Neither believed that psychotherapists should provide interpretations during therapy.
    d. Neither believed that people are rational or socialized.

39. Which of the following viewpoints argues that lower socioeconomic groups show a greater incidence of maladaptive behavior because people who do not function well tend to experience downward mobility?

d

    a. existential
    b. community
    c. social-causation
    d. social-selection

40. _____ occurs whenever people are categorized on some basis, whether that basis is relevant and fair or not.

a. Labeling
b. Social role development
c. Diagnostic classification
d. Mediation

41. By an integrative approach, the authors of your text mean

a. that behavior is a function of several factors.
b. that the brain has primary influence on behavior.
c. that each system of psychotherapy has importance depending on the disorder under consideration.
d. that the best approach to treating mental illness is through a combination of drugs and psychotherapy.

TRUE/FALSE QUESTIONS

Indicate whether each statement is true or false. Check your answers at the end of this chapter.

1. At the extreme, the biological perspective assumes all disordered behaviors are due to bodily dysfunctions or defects.

2. Monozygotic twins develop from the same fertilized egg.

3. The somatic nervous system transmits information from sense organs to the muscles.

4. The limbic system is not responsible for motivational or emotional functions.

5. Neuroscientists have shown that behavior, perception and cognition are the results of integrated actions of networks of nerve cells.

6. Psychoneuroimmunology is the study of the effects of drugs on behavior.

7. Freud changed behavior by attempting to identify and eliminate psychic determinants.

8. Saving money for a goal would reflect primary process thinking.

9. One of the goals of psychoanalytic therapy is the elimination of the use of defense mechanisms.

F   10.   Punishment is one of the most common forms of negative reinforcement.

T   11.   Operant conditioning deals with responses that occur relatively infrequently prior to being reinforced.

T   12.   The cognitive view seeks to account for behavior by studying the ways in which the person uses available information.

F   13.   George Kelly supported the view that the greater part of mental life is hidden in the unconscious.

T   14.   Ellis regards intense emotions and maladaptive behavior as the consequence of irrational thoughts.

F   15.   The community perspective suggests that psychological problems are closely related to problems existing only within the individual.

T   16.   The interactional approach suggests that the way a situation influences behavior depends on the particular capabilities of an individual experiencing a particular set of conditions.

MATCHING

Match the following terms with the information provided below. The answers may be found at the end of this chapter.

a. antigens
b. genome
c. preconscious
d. escape response
e. secondary process thinking
f. object relations
g. phallic psychosexual stage

h. classical conditioning
i. schedule
j. intervening variable
k. stressor
l. karyotypes
m. conditioned response
n. substantia nigra
o. population genetics

_n_   site in brain associated with Parkinson's disease
_k_   condition that makes it difficult to maintain biological and psychological adaptation
_l_   maps of chromosomes
_i_   basis for reinforcement
_e_   allows for the delay of gratification
_h_   model used by Pavlov with his dogs
_c_   contains information which may readily become conscious

<u>m</u> a behavior which is learned to be associated with a particular stimulus
<u>d</u> involves the use of an aversive US
<u>a</u> foreign materials
<u>f</u> the mind is composed of internal representations of significant others
<u>b</u> complete set of a person's genes
<u>g</u> pleasure is associated with the genitals
<u>i</u> inferred variable
<u>o</u> study of gene distributions in groups of individuals

ANSWER KEY

Multiple Choice

1. B	22. D
2. A	23. C
3. C	24. B
4. D	25. B
5. C	26. B
6. C	27. D
7. A	28. B
8. D	29. D
9. C	30. A
10. B	31. A
11. D	32. D
12. A	33. C
13. D	34. D
14. A	35. C
15. B	36. B
16. D	37. C
17. C	38. B
18. D	39. D
19. D	40. A
20. C	41. A
21. A	

True/False

1. T	9. F
2. T	10. F
3. T	11. T
4. F	12. T
5. T	13. F
6. F	14. T
7. T	15. F
8. F	16. T

Matching

n
k
l
I
e
h
c
m
d
a
f
b
g
j
o

Chapter 4
CLASSIFICATION AND ASSESSMENT

CHAPTER OVERVIEW

This chapter presents various methods for classifying and assessing abnormal behaviors. The currently used diagnostic system, The Diagnostic and Statistical Manual, 4th edition (DSM-IV) is described. The five axes of the DSM are discussed and examples are presented. Various methods for assessing individuals are highlighted including: interviews, psychological tests, behavioral assessment, cognitive assessment, relational assessment, and bodily assessment.

CHAPTER OUTLINE

Classification: Categories of Maladaptive Behavior
        Advantages and Disadvantages of Classification
        Vulnerability, Resiliency, and Coping
        The Multiaxial Approach
        DSM-IV
        The Major Diagnostic Categories
        Evaluation of the DSM Multiaxial Approach
        Research on Classification

Assessment: The Basis of Classification
        The Interview
        Intelligence Tests
        Personality Assessment
        Behavioral Assessment
        Cognitive Assessment
        Relational Assessment
        Bodily Assessment

LEARNING OBJECTIVES

You should know:

1.   the purpose of having a multiaxial classification system in the DSM, and what the five axes of the system are.

2. what general types of information are sought during an assessment interview, and the differences between a diagnostic and a therapeutic interview.

3. the types of information yielded by the Wechsler tests that make them more popular than the Binet test.

4. the rationale for the construction of the K-ABC, its division into sequential and simultaneous processing subtests, and its use with minority children.

5. the sort of information that may be included in a psychological report based on a testing session.

6. how the MMPI clinical scales were developed and how the MMPI is used in clinical practice.

7. how rating scales are used and some of their methodological problems.

8. the rationale underlying the use of projective techniques, as well as the materials, administration procedures, and general interpretational goals of the Rorschach, TAT, sentence completion, and word-association methods.

9. how behavioral assessment differs from more traditional forms of assessment, and the goals of conducting a behavior assessment and the kinds of questions asked in doing so.

10. what cognitive assessment is and how it is carried out.

11. the rationale underlying relational assessment and how it is conducted.

12. some of the bodily functions measured through bodily assessment, and some advantages and limitation of this form of assessment.

KEY TERMS AND CONCEPTS

Following is a list of key terms and concepts that are featured in the chapter and are important for you to know. Write out the definitions of each of these terms and check your answer with definitions in the text.

diagnosis
DSM-IV
multiaxial classification system
global assessment of functioning
reliability
Kappa statistic
validity

assessment interview
diagnostic interview
therapeutic interview
structured interview
standardized interview
Diagnostic Interview Schedule
structured clinical interview
Binet Tests
Wechsler Tests
Verbal IQ
Performance IQ
Full Scale IQ
WISC-R
WPPSI
K-ABC
personality inventories
MMPI
rating scales
Behavior Rating Scale for Children
Visual Analogue Scale
halo effect
projective techniques
Rorschach Inkblots
TAT
word association test
sentence completion test
behavioral assessment
baseline observations
operant observations
cognitive assessment
relational assessment
bodily assessment
galvanic skin response
polygraph
biofeedback
brain imaging techniques

CRITICAL THINKING QUESTIONS

In developing answers for the following questions, turn to that section of your chapter that covers the pertinent materials. Read the section thoroughly before attempting to frame your answer.

1.   How is classification used? In what ways is classification useful?

2. What are the major sources of diagnostic unreliability?

3. What is the DSM? Describe the five axes.

4. What is the relationship between Axis I and Axis II diagnostic categories?

5. List the major differences between earlier and later versions of the DSM.

6. Explain why reliability and validity are important concepts in classification. List the factors that influence clinical judgment.

7. What are the major assessment methods used in gathering information about clients?

8. Describe the two types of clinical interviews. What are the general types of information sought during an interview? List the 4 components of the clinical interview.

9. What are the Binet and Wechsler tests? Explain the concept of intelligence/IQ as measured by these tests.

10. Briefly describe the dimensions that are assessed using the MMPI-2. How are the L, F and K scales used?

11. What impact does the "halo effect" have on rating scales?

12. What is the rationale underlying the use of projective tests?

13. What are the goals of behavioral assessment? What questions are of interest to the clinician?

14. Explain cognitive assessment.

15. Why would a clinician be interested in making a relational assessment?

16. What is measured during bodily assessment?

17. The concept of "IQ" and its measurement has been a topic of debate for many years. Proponents of IQ assessment believe it is a useful device, while those against it argue that it is a form of "labeling" and derived from tests that are culturally biased. What is your position on this topic? Support it.

MULTIPLE CHOICE

The following multiple choice questions will test your comprehension of the material presented in the chapter. Circle the correct choice for each question in the section, then compare your answers with those at the end of the chapter.

1. A classification statement that places a disorder within a system of conventional groupings is called a/an

    a. axis.
    b. diagnosis.
    c. interview.
    d. clinical judgment.

2. Two major sources of diagnostic unreliability are

    a. differences in training of therapists and the stigma associated with labeling an individual.
    b. the stigma associated with labeling and the lack of training of many professionals who do diagnostic interviews.
    c. differences in the training of therapists and the uniqueness of every individual.
    d. the uniqueness of every individual and the stigma associated with placing labels on individuals.

3. A good clinical classification system provides for causes of a condition, a common language for communication, a short- and long-term outlook, and

    a. considers the contribution of genetics.
    b. gives a low kappa statistics.
    c. shows low validity but high reliability.
    d. provides clues for treatment and prevention.

4. A multiaxial classification system gives the clinician an opportunity to

    a. provide a single label for the various dimensions of a person's psychological problems.
    b. describe an individual along several dimensions.
    c. decrease reliability while maximizing validity.
    d. select the single best description of maladaptive behavior and explain the behavior's etiology.

5.   The first three axes of the DSM classification system contain

    a. case history information.
    b. a description of the symptoms and estimation about how long it will take for the person to improve with therapy.
    c. the probable cause of the disorder and suggestions for the best type of therapy and medications to use.
    d. diagnostic categories and general medical information.

6.   Which of the following is not included in the Axis I categories?

    a. disorders of infancy and childhood
    b. sleep disorders
    c. sexual disorders
    d. mental retardation

7.   Both DSM-III and DSM-IV have increased the reliability of diagnosis by

    a. providing a theoretical orientation for each disorder.
    b. reducing the sheer volume of information contained in the manuals.
    c. emphasizing descriptions of behavior.
    d. decreasing coverage of the range of disorders.

8.   A major criticism of earlier versions of DSM lies in their

    a. reliance on statistical data.
    b. inability to accurately diagnose problems of childhood.
    c. unreliability of categories due to hypothesizing about underlying causes.
    d. use of multiple axes.

9.   Which of the following is not a criticism of recent DSMs?

    a. Insufficient attention is paid to prior history.
    b. Too few field trials have been conducted on the categories to convince clinicians that these categories are stable.
    c. It has not been coordinated with the ICD.
    d. Consistency of diagnosis decreases when clinicians attempt to make distinctions in classification within the finer subdivisions of the general categories.

10.   _____ refers to the diagnostic agreement among clinicians as to a particular individual.

    a. Reliability
    b. Stability
    c. Validity
    d. Cohesion

11. Which of the following is not implicated in the error of clinical research?

    a. Clinician factors
    b. Criteria factors
    c. Age factors
    d. Method factors

_c_

12. The purpose of the assessment interview is to

    a. modify maladaptive behaviors.
    b. identify problems and determine the nature of maladaptive behaviors.
    c. explain to the client the origins of his/her problems.
    d. identify the traumatic childhood events, which form the roots of present problems.

_b_

13. Select the statement that is true of cross-cultural research on maladaptive behavior.

    a. Regardless of the cultural setting, the expression of depression is the same.
    b. The experience of depression as an intrapsychic experience is universal.
    c. Rates of depression are higher in European countries than in the U.S.
    d. Asian Americans somaticize depression.

_d_

14. The concept of behavioral observations refers to

    a. the notion that a behavior must be observable in order to be significant.
    b. how a client perceives the therapist's behavior.
    c. observing the manner in which a client behaves.
    d. the use of physiological recording devices to measure a behavior.

_c_

15. Of the following, which characteristic of an interviewer might readily influence the course and content of an interview?

    a. gender
    b. hair color
    c. height
    d. manner of dress

_a_

16. A psychologist would use the Diagnostic Interview Schedule (DIS) during

    a. an unstructured interview.
    b. psychoanalysis.
    c. a standardized interview.
    d. personality assessment.

_c_

17. _____ were the first widely recognized psychological assessment tool.

    a. Intelligence Tests
    b. Personality Inventories
    c. Rating Scales
    d. The Diagnostic Interview Schedules

18. The Wechsler tests differ from the Binet tests in that the Wechsler tests provide

    a. a score for mental age.
    b. a verbal and performance IQ score.
    c. an IQ score for chronological ability.
    d. information about personality disorders.

19. The K-ABC's reported strength over other intelligence tests for children lies in its

    a. length.
    b. attempt to reduce cultural bias.
    c. reliance on verbal responses.
    d. ease of administration.

20. The most widely used personality inventory is the

    a. Thematic Apperception Test.
    b. WAIS-R.
    c. Rorschach Inkblot Test.
    d. MMPI.

21. The L, F, and K scales of the MMPI were designed to evaluate

    a. lethargy, fantasy, and kleptomaniac tendencies.
    b. impulses toward antisocial behaviors.
    c. bizarre thinking, delusions, and hallucinations.
    d. honesty, carelessness, and defensiveness.

22. The major contribution of the MMPI-2 over the MMPI lies in

    a. the former's deletion of culturally sensitive items.
    b. the addition of the K-scale.
    c. three new scales to measure reliability.
    d. none of the above

23. Johnny is a 7 year old who experiences problems of impulsivity in class. Which of the following tests would most likely be selected by a school psychologist to evaluate Johnny's problem?

    a. Behavior Rating Scale for Children
    b. Children's Visual Analogue Scale
    c. TAT
    d. Rorschach

24. An individual comes to a clinic complaining of chronic backache. In order to evaluate this condition, a clinician would most probably administer the

    a. Visual Analogue Scale.
    b. Thematic Apperception Test.
    c. Rorschach.
    d. sentence completion technique.

25. Defense mechanisms, latent impulses, and anxieties have all been inferred from data gathered in

    a. projective situations.
    b. rating scale interviews.
    c. neuropsychological tests.
    d. behavioral assessment.

26. A patient reports, "It looks like an apple tree in the middle of a huge forest...and there's my mother lying on the ground under it. She was hit in the head by an apple while picking them. Hey, this is fun, it's like looking at clouds and seeing figures." Which of the following tests was the patient most probably taking?

    a. MMPI-2
    b. Rorschach Inkblot
    c. Thematic Apperception Test
    d. none of the above

27. A word association test is an example of

    a. an unstructured interview.
    b. a projective intelligence test.
    c. a projective technique.
    d. a cognitive assessment.

28.   Counting the number of times a young child hits other playmates is characteristics of

   a. cognitive assessment.
   b. behavioral assessment.
   c. bodily assessment.
   d. aggression assessment.

29.   Cognitive assessment provides information about

   a. anxieties and insecurities.
   b. distortions in thinking that play a role in psychological problems.
   c. repressed wishes and conflicts stemming from early childhood traumas.
   d. latent impulses.

30.   The Quality of Relationships Inventory is an example of a _____ instrument.

   a. projective
   b. baseline assessment
   c. behavioral assessment
   d. relational assessment

31.   Which of the following is true regarding the polygraph?

   a. It measures feelings of guilt.
   b. It measures truthfulness.
   c. It measures level of interest in a subject.
   d. It measures physiological reactions.

TRUE/FALSE QUESTIONS

Indicate whether each statement is true or false. Check your answers at the end of this chapter.

1.   The most widely accepted classification system for abnormal behavior is the DSM.

2.   Axis I refers to any physiological disorder that is relevant to the condition of a client.

3.   DSM-I and DSM-II are criticized for focusing too heavily on psychoanalytic theory.

4.   Since the advent of DSM-III, schizophrenia has been diagnosed less frequently.

5.   A diagnosis is a product of present knowledge and opinion about abnormal behavior.

F   6.   Although the validity of DSM-IV has been established, the reliability of its categories remains questionable.

F   7.   Typically, the clinician relies on a single assessment tool in gathering information about a client.

F   8.   The ability to quickly size up a situation and plan a treatment strategy based on the assessment is not particularly important as a clinical skill.

F   9.   An advantage of the Binet Intelligence Test is that it provides both Verbal IQ and Performance IQ scores.

T   10.   Baseline observations are records of response frequencies taken in order to evaluate the effectiveness of a therapeutic technique.

T   11.   Cognitive assessment attempts to identify thoughts and ideas.

MATCHING

Match the following with information presented below. The answers can be found at the end of the chapter.

a. Verbal IQ
b. Axis III
c. cognitive assessment
d. WPPSI
e. biofeedback
f. TAT

g. Axis V
h. Behavior Rating Scale for Children
i. operant observations
j. Kappa statistic
k. mental age

___b___ refers to physical disorders
___j___ measure of reliability
___c___ provides information about thoughts
___g___ global assessment of functioning
___d___ intelligence test for children
___i___ recording of response frequencies
___e___ provides a continuous recording of physiological measures
___f___ requires client to make-up a story
___a___ measure provided by a Wechsler test
___h___ measures a child's degree of self-control
___k___ construct developed by Binet

51

ANSWER KEY

Multiple Choice

1. B	17. A
2. C	18. B
3. D	19. B
4. B	20. D
5. D	21. D
6. D	22. D
7. C	23. A
8. C	24. A
9. C	25. A
10. A	26. B
11. C	27. C
12. B	28. B
13. D	29. B
14. C	30. D
15. A	31. D
16. C	

True/False

1. T	7. F
2. F	8. F
3. T	9. F
4. T	10. T
5. T	11. T
6. F	

Matching

b
j
c
g
d
i
e
f
a
h
k

Chapter 5
STRESS, COPING, AND MALADAPTIVE BEHAVIOR

CHAPTER OVERVIEW

This chapter reviews the role of stress in contributing to maladaptive behavior. Various stress-arousing situations and stressful life transitions are discussed and coping techniques are evaluated. Failures of coping with stress that lead to adjustment disorders, posttraumatic stress disorders, and the dissociative disorders are presented. Therapeutic techniques for dealing with stressful situations are explored.

CHAPTER OUTLINE

Stress and Coping
> Coping Skills
> Social Support

Stressful Situations and Life Transitions
> Stress-Arousing Situations
> Life Transitions

Clinical Reactions to Stress
> Adjustment Disorder
> Posttraumatic Stress Disorder
> Dissociative Disorder

Treating Stress-Related Problems
> Supportive Therapy
> Drugs and Sedatives
> Relaxation Training
> Systematic Desensitization
> Cognitive Modification
> Social Intervention

LEARNING OBJECTIVES

You should know:

1.   the factors that influence a person's vulnerability to stress.

2.   coping techniques that are effective with stressors.

3.   the role social support plays in coping with stress.

4.   the psychological, bodily, and behavioral reactions to stress.

5.   the characteristics of stress-arousing situations.

6.   examples of situations that lead to very high stress levels.

7.   the characteristics of adjustment disorders.

8.   the characteristics of posttraumatic stress disorder.

9.   the characteristics of the dissociative disorders.

10.   how therapy techniques are applied to stress-related problems.

KEY TERMS AND CONCEPTS

Following is a list of key terms and concepts that are featured in the chapter and are important for you to know. Write out the definitions of each of these terms and check your answers with the definitions in the text.

vulnerability
temperament
coping skills
social support
adjustment disorder
bereavement
grief
posttraumatic stress disorder
acute stress disorder
dissociative disorder
dissociative amnesia
localized amnesia
select amnesia
general amnesia

continuous amnesia
systematized amnesia
dissociative fugue
dissociative identity disorder
depersonalization

CRITICAL THINKING QUESTIONS

In developing answers for the following questions, turn to that section of your chapter that covers the pertinent material. Read the section thoroughly before attempting to frame your answer.

1. How is a person's vulnerability to stress influenced by temperament, coping skills and social support?

2. Stress-arousing conditions fall into two broad categories: traumatic events/personal crises and developmental transitions. List typical stressors for each category. What psychological, bodily and behavioral responses might a person experience as a result of these stressors?

3. Adjustment disorders, posttraumatic stress disorders and dissociative disorders are all maladaptive attempts to cope with stress. Compare and contrast these disorders.

4. Date rape is a very serious concern on college campuses today. Briefly discuss its dimensions and the results of research efforts in this area.

5. What are the therapeutic techniques used in treating stress-related disorders? How does each intervention attempt to aid the person in coping?

6. The diagnosis of dissociative identity disorder is a controversial one. Many people believe that this disorder is simply faked by the individual. What is your position on this matter? Defend it.

MULTIPLE CHOICE

The following multiple choice questions will test your comprehension of the material presented in the chapter. Circle the correct choice for each question in the section, then compare your answers with those at the end of the chapter.

1. A person's _____ is influenced by his or her temperament, coping skills, and the social support available.

    a. primary appraisal
    b. secondary appraisal

c. vulnerability to stress
d. task orientation

2. Temperament is best described as

a. changing from situation to situation.
b. an outgrowth of early childhood experience.
c. the energy level of response, irrespective of its quality.
d. consistent aspects of behavior, especially those related to feelings and emotions.

3. Which of the following is FALSE about using coping techniques when dealing with a stressful situation?

a. Different coping strategies are effective in different types of situations.
b. What you don't know can't hurt you.
c. Successful copers have a varied array of personal resources for coping with situations.
d. Successful copers have the ability to use humor to defuse a situation.

4. Which of the following is not considered to be a personal resource for coping?

a. considering alternatives
b. keeping your concern to yourself
c. using humor
d. redefining a situation

5. Which of the following is an example of a reinforcing self-statement used when dealing with a stressful situation?

a. "I'm not going to worry about what happens."
b. "I'll take things one step at a time."
c. "I didn't handle that very well--just like usual."
d. "I really did a good job handling that one."

6. Which of the following statements is FALSE regarding the effects of social support on one's ability to deal with stressful situations?

a. People should learn to be independent and not count on family or friends to help them.
b. People who have high levels of social support are less vulnerable to illness than those with few social supports.
c. There appears to be no minimum number of social supports that ensures satisfaction for everyone.
d. People who are low in social support tend to be perceived by others as less interesting than people who are high in social support.

7.   Select a characteristic below that is not a typical bodily response to stress.

c

   a. rapid pulse
   b. pounding heart
   c. increased or decreased sleeping
   d. increased perspiration

8.   Research has shown that

b

   a. recent stressors exert less influence than past stressors on our lives.
   b. the experience of multiple stressors in the recent past is related to increased risk for depression and anxiety.
   c. at the present, there are not measures to assess the severity and perceptions of stressors.
   d. both a and c

9.   Stress-arousing situations vary along several dimensions. These include: severity, degree of loss of control, the individual's level of self-confidence, suddenness, and

c

   a. predictability; generality.
   b. susceptibility; generality.
   c. predictability; duration.
   d. duration; sensitivity.

10.   Witnessing a traumatic event such as an airplane crash may cause the observer

b

   a. to suffer immediate effects but no long-term effects.
   b. to suffer long-range problems as well as immediate effects.
   c. to suffer a psychological stress reaction but not a bodily one.
   d. to suffer emotional stress only.

11.   Which of the following is FALSE of date rape?

c

   a. The most prevalent fears for victims include being alone, going out, darkness and encountering strangers.
   b. College women are a high risk group for date rape.
   c. Alcohol and drug use are not major contributing factors to nonconsensual sex.
   d. Typically, physical force is not used.

12.   According to Sanders (1993), which of the following is a high risk factor for poor outcome of bereavement?

d

   a. emotional dependence on the deceased
   b. death of a child

c. chronic illness

d. being a widower

13. Select the aspect below that is not typically seen in bereavement.

c

a. crying

b. social withdrawal

c. suicidal ideation

d. anxiety

14. An adjustment disorder

d

a. is often part of a lifelong pattern of maladaptive behavior.

b. usually involves extremely bizarre behavior.

c. is generally in direct proportion to the severity of the stressor; more severe stressors produce more severe adjustment disorders.

d. involves poor adaptation to one or more stressors that have occurred in the previous three months.

15. Select the following statement(s) that is(are) true of adjustment disorders.

d

a. Typical behaviors seen include truancy and reckless driving.

b. The individual is expected to return to pre-stressor functioning within 6 months.

c. War veterans are not likely to suffer this disorder.

d. Both a & b

16. The difference between PTSD and acute stress disorder lies in the

a

a. time of onset of the symptoms

b. age of the client

c. nature of the stressor

d. all of the above

17. According to Koopman and others (1994), people who _____ in an emergency may be more prone to experience PTSD.

c

a. react with a startle response

b. react with immediate fear

c. react to the stressor with unwarranted calm

d. solicit the help of others

18. Choose the following statement that is true.

d

a. Dissociative disorders tend to have gradual onsets.

b. Dissociative disorders tend to last only a brief period.

c. People suffering from dissociative disorders have a difficult time getting rid of the memories of the traumatic event.

d. Dissociative disorders usually begin in childhood.

19. Which of the following associations is correct?

a. Selective amnesia--entire life is forgotten

b. Continuous amnesia--events during a particular period of time

c. Localized amnesia--events during a particular period of time

d. Generalized amnesia--memory for specific categories of information

20. A week after being fired from his job of 25 years, a husband does not recognize his wife or children. This man is most probably suffering from

a. systematized amnesia.

b. dissociative fugue.

c. dissociative identity disorder.

d. selective amnesia.

21. As dissociative disorders, fugue and amnesia have the following in common.

a. physical flight

b. Both involve behaviors similar to PTSD.

c. The stressor remains conscious.

d. The onset may be sudden or gradual.

22. As a process, dissociation may be viewed as

a. a severing of the connections between various emotions and ideas.

b. part of the psychotic process.

c. inherently pathological.

d. a phenomenon that is restricted to the U.S.

23. A 25-year-old woman was found wandering the local interstate highway. Upon being taken to the local police station, the woman was not able to provide details as to her identity, address, etc. It was later revealed that the woman lived in a town 100 miles away and was last seen at the funeral of her only child. This woman was most probably suffering from

a. dissociative identity disorder.

b. dissociative fugue.

c. dissociative amnesia.

d. depersonalization.

24. Dissociative identity disorder

    a. is seldom psychogenic.
    b. tends to occur more frequently in males than in females.
    c. is seldom tied to early childhood trauma.
    d. occurs very rarely.

25. Identify the statement below that is incorrect.

    a. DID is a rare disorder.
    b. Males experience DID 4 times more frequently than females.
    c. In DID, the person may have alternate personalities that are different genders.
    d. Alternates often have different value systems and handwritings.

26. _____ may be leading to the under diagnosing of dissociative identity disorder.

    a. The patient's attempts to hide alternate personalities
    b. The clinician's unfamiliarity with alternate personalities
    c. The concurrent diagnosis of schizophrenia
    d. The failure of DSM-IV to be explicit regarding the symptoms of DID

27. A person says to a therapist, "I feel as though I'm in a dream, like I'm doing this mechanically." This statement would be most characteristic of someone experiencing

    a. PTSD.
    b. dissociative amnesia.
    c. depersonalization.
    d. dissociative fugue.

28. Which of the following would NOT be part of systematic desensitization training?

    a. focusing attention on specific muscle groups
    b. telling oneself to relax and releasing tension
    c. constructing a hierarchy of anxiety-producing stimuli
    d. attempting to contact alternate personalities

29. Which of the following therapies involves learning new internal dialogues?

    a. relaxation training
    b. systematic desensitization
    c. social intervention
    d. cognitive modification

30.   _____ might typically involve the social worker going into the home to observe familial interactions.

C

a. Reality therapy
b. Cognitive family therapy
c. Social intervention
d. Familial intervention

TRUE/FALSE QUESTIONS

Indicate whether each statement is true or false. Check your answers at the end of this chapter.

T   1.   Past experiences influence the level of stress we experience in a situation and how we cope with it.

T   2.   People sometimes fail to cope effectively with stress because of their high level of arousal.

F   3.   The most stressful aspect of hospitalization for people is the pain often associated with illness and treatment.

F   4.   Research with the Social Support Questionnaire has failed to demonstrate a relationship between social support and physical illness.

T   5.   People who have experienced multiple stressors in the recent past are especially susceptible to depression.

T   6.   College women are a high risk group for sexual assault.

T   7.   Dissociative identity disorder was formerly called multiple personality disorder.

F   8.   PTSD is the same thing as an acute stress disorder.

F   9.   PTSD is less common than thought previously.

F   10. Drug therapies are more effective in treating PTSD than psychotherapy.

F   11. Therapists find it easy to be supportive of clients with dissociative identity disorder.

T   12. Cognitive modification involves learning new internal dialogues and new ways of thinking about situations.

MATCHING

Match the following terms with information provided below. The answers may be found at the end of the chapter.

a. supportive therapy
b. denial
c. PTSD
d. vulnerability
e. social support

f. social intervention
g. bereavement
h. dissociative disorder
i. grief
j. Dissociative identity disorder

_b_ defense mechanism used to cope with bodily symptoms
_j_ involves disparate self-concepts
_h_ usually occurs after childhood with a history of serious family turmoil
_i_ may be accompanied by a sense of numbness and disbelief
_f_ treatment involving family members
_e_ the feeling of being cared about and loved by others
_d_ increases the likelihood of a maladaptive response to stress
_g_ loss of a loved one
_a_ therapist is non-critical
_c_ symptoms may include flashbacks

ANSWER KEY

Multiple Choice

1. A	16. A
2. D	17. C
3. B	18. D
4. B	19. C
5. A	20. D
6. A	21. D
7. C	22. A
8. B	23. B
9. C	24. D
10. B	25. B
11. C	26. A
12. D	27. C
13. C	28. D
14. D	29. D
15. D	30. C

True/False

1. T
2. T
3. F
4. F
5. T
6. T

7. T
8. F
9. F
10. F
11. F
12. T

Matching

b
j
h
i
f
e
d
g
a
c

Chapter 6
PSYCHOLOGICAL FACTORS AND PHYSICAL SYMPTOMS

CHAPTER OVERVIEW

The present chapter investigates the role of psychological, social and bodily systems in the development of physical illness. A biopsychosocial model of illness is presented and the impact of stress on physical functioning is highlighted. The text reviews several psychophysiological disorders, and distinguishes these from somatoform and factitious disorders.

CHAPTER OUTLINE

Psychological, Social, and Bodily Interactions
       The Biopsychosocial Model
       Stress and Illness

Psychophysiological Disorders
       Headaches
       Cardiovascular Disorders
       Cancer
       Asthma

Somatoform Disorders
       Somatization Disorder
       Conversion Disorders
       Hypochondriasis
       Body Dysmorphic Disorder
       Pain Disorders

Factitious Disorders and Malingering

LEARNING OBJECTIVES

You should know:

1.   the characteristics of the psychophysiological approach.

2.   the biopsychosocial model and what homeostasis is.

3. the role of stress in illness and health; how behavioral medicine and health psychology function to keep people healthier.

4. the differentiating features of the three main kinds of headaches and how biofeedback is used in treating them.

5. the relevance to coronary heart disease of cultural factors, stressful events, and community and personal lifestyle. The differences between Type A and Type B personalities and results of research on them.

6. how relaxation training is used to treat hypertension.

7. the psychological factors tentatively implicated in the occurrence of cancer and asthma.

8. the defining characteristics of pain disorder, hypochondriasis, and somatization disorders.

9. the nature of conversion disorders and the dynamics that underlie them.

10. the difference between factitious disorders and malingering; what Munchausen's syndrome is.

KEY TERMS AND CONCEPTS

Following is a list of key terms and concepts that are featured in the chapter and are important for you to know. Write out the definitions of each of these terms and check your answers with the definitions in the text.

psychosomatic disorder
psychophysiological disorder
somatoform disorder
factitious disorder
psychosomatic hypothesis
biopsychosocial model
homeostasis
behavioral medicine
health psychology
muscle contraction headaches
tension headaches
migraine headaches
aura
cluster headaches

biofeedback
cardiovascular disorders
coronary heart disease
plaques
angina pectoris
atherosclerosis
myocardial infarction
catecholamine
epinephrine
norepinephrine
Type A
Type B
hypertension
allergen
asthma
Briquet's syndrome
hypochondriasis
glove anesthesia
somatization disorder
conversion disorder
body dysmorphic disorder
pain disorder
A-B-A-B design
Munchausen syndrome
malingering

CRITICAL THINKING QUESTIONS

In developing answers for the following questions, turn to the section of your chapter that covers the pertinent material. Read the section thoroughly before attempting to frame your answer.

1.   What is the psychosomatic hypothesis?

2.   Describe the interactive nature of the effects of biological and psychosocial factors on health. Explain the Biopsychosocial Model of Health.

3.   What psychological skills appear to decrease a person's risk for illness?

4.   What are the similarities and differences between behavioral medicine and health psychology?

5.   What is a psychophysiological disorder?

6. Compare and contrast muscle contraction, migraine and cluster headaches.

7. What is biofeedback and how is it used in behavioral medicine? What does research say about its effectiveness?

8. What are the biological and psychological variables relating to coronary heart disease? What are the sociocultural factors associated with coronary heart disease?

9. What are the characteristics of the Type A coronary-prone person? Discuss the findings of the Framingham study.

10. Describe the factors associated with hypertension.

11. What are some psychological factors that might be associated with cancer?

12. How may psychological factors influence the severity of asthma?

13. Describe the somatoform disorders, listing key characteristics.

14. Briefly explain the factors involved in the factitious disorders. What is the difference between a factitious disorder and malingering?

MULTIPLE CHOICE

The following multiple choice questions will test your comprehension of the material presented in the chapter. Circle the correct choice for each question in the section, then compare your answers with those at the end of the chapter.

1. According to Kennedy and others (1990),

   a. the quantity of close relationships has an effect on the immune system.
   b. the quality of our social support network influences the functioning of our immune system.
   c. although intuitively reasonable, there is no relationship between social support and immune system functioning.
   d. none of the above.

2. Bodily symptoms may be caused by blocking of emotional expression according to the

   a. psychosomatic hypothesis.
   b. general adaptation syndrome.
   c. biopsychosocial model.
   d. organ susceptibility hypothesis.

3.   The _____ releases hormones under "flight or fight" conditions.

   a. adrenal medulla
   b. adrenal cortex
   c. pituitary system
   d. brain

4.   Malarkey and others (1994) have established that there are hormonal and blood pressure changes under conflict conditions in

   a. married couples.
   b. separated couples.
   c. divorced couples.
   d. both a & c.

5.   Which of the following is FALSE regarding the biopsychosocial model?

   a. A person can be regarded as a system with interacting subsystems.
   b. Biopsychosocial problems occur when a person's life is disrupted.
   c. Illness is due mostly to the influence of external agents.
   d. The biopsychosocial model is relevant to the prevention and treatment of illness.

6.   Health psychology is concerned with

   a. rehabilitation.
   b. diagnosis and treatment.
   c. promoting mental health.
   d. disease prevention.

7.   Which of the following skills appears to be directly related to a decreased risk of illness?

   a. ability to remain inflexible in the face of change
   b. ability to be "stoic" and suppress feelings
   c. ability to deny circumstances
   d. ability to form loving relationships

8.   Stress

   a. stimulates hormonal secretions.
   b. induces biochemical changes.
   c. alters the brain's electrical level.
   d. all of the above.

9.   The term _____ has been applied to physical conditions in which psychologically meaningful events are closely related to bodily symptoms.

       a. biofeedback
       b. longevity
       c. hardiness
       d. psychophysiological

10.   Psychophysiological disorders include disorders of the

       a. cardiovascular system.
       b. brain.
       c. skin.
       d. both a and c.

11.   The three components of headache pain are physiological changes, subjective experience of pain, and

       a. duration of pain.
       b. behavior motivated by the pain.
       c. intensity of pain.
       d. both a and c.

12.   A friend of yours is describing a psychophysiological disorder to you. When she mentions experiencing an "aura", you know she is referring to her

       a. cancer treatments.
       b. hypertension.
       c. migraine headaches.
       d. factitious disorder.

13.   According to Breslau and Davis (1993), many migraine sufferers experience

       a. depression.
       b. isolation.
       c. anxiety.
       d. both a and c.

14.   Cluster headaches

       a. are more frequent in women.
       b. are often confined to one side of the head.
       c. rarely occur at night.
       d. tend not to be severely painful.

15. Through _____ we can become aware of our autonomic responses.

   a. sensitivity training
   b. endocrine training
   c. ECT
   d. biofeedback

16. The number one cause of death and disability in the United States is

   a. asthma.
   b. coronary heart disease.
   c. cancer.
   d. none of the above.

17. Myocardial infarction

   a. is rare in the elderly.
   b. is the least lethal of CHD types.
   c. is the same as a "heart attack".
   d. is directly associated with over exercise.

18. Factors known to increase the risk of CHD include age, cigarette smoking, high blood pressure and

   a. diabetes.
   b. liver disease.
   c. occupation.
   d. migraines.

19. In a study by Kowacki and others (1994), it was found that highly anxious men are _____ times more likely to suffer sudden cardiac deaths than less anxious men.

   a. 6
   b. 10
   c. 4
   d. 2

20. A study evaluating the effects of life style on coronary heart disease risk in identical twins (Liljefors & Rahe, 1970) found that

   a. genetics proved to be the best predictor of the disease.
   b. diet was directly related to coronary heart disease.
   c. life-style was an important factor in the disease.
   d. both b & c.

21. Friedman and Rosenman (1974) found that

    a. there is little difference in risk for CHD between type A and type B personalities.
    b. Type B had twice the risk for CHD than type A.
    c. Type B personalities tended to be competitive and hostile.
    d. none of the above.

22. A recent study using husbands' and wives' ratings of hostility (Kneip et al., 1993) found

    a. the higher the spouse-rated hostility, the higher the likelihood of CHD.
    b. the higher the spouse-rated hostility, the lower the likelihood of CHD.
    c. no relationship between hostility and risk of CHD.
    d. that wives were not accurate in assessing their husbands' latent hostility.

23. Choose the following statement which is true.

    a. There is no cultural differences in rates of CHD.
    b. Japan and the U.S. have the highest rates of CHD.
    c. Japan has the highest rate for CHD of all countries studied.
    d. None of the above.

24. _____ and _____ have been identified as important factors in the development of hypertension.

    a. chronic anger; anger suppression
    b. hostility; passivity
    c. chronic anger; explosive behavior
    d. passivity; denial

25. Glaser and Kiecolt-Glaser (1994)

    a. have demonstrated that stress reduction enhances immune system functioning.
    b. failed to show a relationship between stress reactions and immune functioning.
    c. believe there is no relationship between stress reactions and immune functioning.
    d. none of the above.

26. Benson's (1977) method for developing relaxation involves four elements: a repetitive mental device, a passive attitude, a quiet environment, and

    a. increased muscle tension.
    b. music.
    c. a relaxed attitude.
    d. decreased muscle tension.

27. Research suggests that _____ may help people with cancer become better copers.

a. biofeedback
b. individual counseling
c. group psychotherapy
d. a belief in God

28. One study investigating the home environments of asthmatic children (Purcel et al., 1969) found

a. no relationship between home and asthma.
b. the parents to be over controlling and the environment tense.
c. that removing the children from their home environments resulted in no change in conditions.
d. none of the above.

29. Which of the following is not a statement that a somatizer might make.

a. "I really can't take it much longer."
b. "I feel as weak as a cat."
c. "I throw-up every evening."
d. "I often feel I'm in the wrong body."

30. Glove anesthesia is an example of a _____ disorder.

a. psychogenic pain
b. conversion
c. hypochondriacal
d. factitious

31. Susan appears to be obsessed by her bodily condition and fears developing a disease. Her behavior is most typical of someone experiencing

a. hypochondriasis.
b. a conversion disorder.
c. a factitious disorder.
d. a conversion disorder.

32. Linda goes to a plastic surgeon complaining of her "ugly and lopsided chin." Upon examination, the surgeon remarked that her chin looked normal and symmetric. If Linda experiences a heightened self-consciousness due to her chin, she would probably be diagnosed as having a(n)

a. conversion disorder.
b. identity disorder.

    c. body dysmorphic disorder.
    d. factitious disorder.

33.   Pain disorders are frequently accompanied by

    a. an inability to attend work.
    b. substantial use of medications.
    c. interpersonal problems.
    d. all of the above.

TRUE/FALSE QUESTIONS

Indicate whether each statement is true or false. Check your answers at the end of this chapter.

1.   The quality of close relationships can influence the functioning of the immune system.

2.   Evidence exists that stress plays an important role in health and illness.

3.   Many of the disorders discussed in this chapter are thought to be the result of prolonged stress.

4.   Homeostasis refers to a state of balance in the body.

5.   Hostility is related to high risk for coronary heart disease.

6.   Cancer is not a single disease.

7.   Deficits in social support are not associated with CHD.

8.   Environmental factors may influence the functioning of the immune system in humans.

9.   The blood pressures of African-American adults tend to exceed those of white adults.

10.   Many students show decreased immune system functioning during exam periods.

11.   It appears that biofeedback training skills are lost soon after training ends.

12.   Exercise has been used to facilitate pain management.

MATCHING

Match the following terms with information provided below. The answers may be found at the end of the chapter.

a.   psychosomatic hypothesis
b.   glove anesthesia
c.   A-B-A-B research design
d.   malingering
e.   epinephrine

f.   Munchausen syndrome
g.   allergen
h.   Type B personality
i.   tension headache
j.   biopsychosocial model

_____ an anatomical impossibility
_____ seeking medical attention to achieve some specific goal
_____ focuses on interaction between 3 variables
_____ one of the catecholamine
_____ physical symptoms result from blocked emotional expression
_____ caused by muscle contractions
_____ a repeated measures design that allows for a subject to act as his own control group
_____ factitious disorder in which person seeks repeated medical evaluations
_____ substance that may cause allergic reactions
_____ less risk for heart disease than A cohorts

ANSWER KEY

Multiple Choice

1. B
2. A
3. A
4. A
5. C
6. D
7. D
8. D
9. D
10. D
11. B
12. C
13. D
14. B
15. D
16. B
17. C

18. A
19. A
20. C
21. D
22. A
23. D
24. A
25. D
26. D
27. C
28. B
29. D
30. B
31. A
32. C
33. D

True/False

1. T
2. T
3. T
4. T
5. T
6. T

7. F
8. T
9. T
10. T
11. T
12. T

Matching
b
d
j
e
a
i
c
f
g
h

Chapter 7
ANXIETY DISORDERS

CHAPTER OVERVIEW

The focus of this chapter is on describing four different types of anxiety disorders that have intense feelings of tension, panic and anxiety at their core. The four types presented are: generalized anxiety disorder, panic disorder, phobic disorder and obsessive-compulsive disorder. These disorders are then discussed from the psychodynamic, learning, cognitive and biological perspectives.

CHAPTER OUTLINE

Generalized Anxiety Disorder

Panic Disorder

Phobias
>   Specific Phobias
>   Social Phobias
>   Agoraphobia

Obsessive-Compulsive Disorder

Interpreting and Treating Anxiety Disorders
The Psychodynamic Perspective
The Behavioral Perspective
The Cognitive Perspective
The Biological Perspective

LEARNING OBJECTIVES

You should know:

1.   the common symptoms and self-descriptions of anxiety.

2.   the four types of symptoms of generalized anxiety disorder.

3.   the defining characteristics of panic attacks and how they differ from generalized anxiety disorder.

4.   the defining characteristics of phobias in general and the current ideas about their etiology and prevalence.

5.   the three general types of phobias and the symptoms of each.

6.   the common features of obsessive-compulsive disorder; how it differs from and resembles phobias; the distinction between obsessions and compulsions.

7.   the psychodynamic view of anxiety disorders and the treatment approach derived from it.

8.   the behavioral view of anxiety disorders and the treatment techniques derived from it, including exposure therapies and modeling.

9.   the cognitive view of anxiety disorders and the treatment strategies derived from it, including cognitive restructuring, thought stopping, cognitive rehearsal, and combinations of cognitive and behavioral rehearsal.

10.   the biological view of anxiety disorders and the treatment methods derived from it, including genetic and environmental factors and drug therapies. Students should know the meaning of comorbidity.

KEY TERMS AND CONCEPTS

Following is a list of key terms and concepts that are featured in the chapter and are important for you to know. Write out the definitions of each of these terms and check your answers with the definitions in the text.

anxiety
anxiety disorders
generalized anxiety disorder
panic disorder
panic attacks
phobic disorder
social phobia
specific phobia
obsessive-compulsive disorder
agoraphobia
obsessive
compulsive
isolation

undoing
reaction formation
behavior therapy
systematic desensitization
implosive therapy
in vivo exposure
flooding
modeling
cognitive behavior therapy
cognitive restructuring
thought stopping
cognitive rehearsal
benzodiazepines
antidepressants
comorbidity

CRITICAL THINKING QUESTIONS

In developing answers for the following questions, turn to the section of your chapter that covers the pertinent material. Read the section thoroughly before attempting to frame your answer.

1. How can anxiety facilitate adaptation? In what way are fear and anxiety different?

2. How do anxiety disorders differ from the simple experience of anxiety?

3. What are the major symptoms most likely to be manifested in a generalized anxiety disorder?

4. What are the differences between generalized anxiety disorders and panic disorders?

5. Define the term "phobia." List its primary characteristics.

6. What are obsessions and compulsions? What are the most common features of obsessive-compulsive disorders?

7. How does the psychodynamic perspective explain anxiety disorders? In what way would a learning perspective explain anxiety disorders?

8. Describe the techniques used in behavior therapy to treat anxiety disorders.

9. How does the cognitive model attempt to explain anxiety disorders? List and explain techniques used by cognitive therapists.

10. How might a person's biological make-up contribute to an anxiety disorder? What treatments are used by this perspective?

11. Do you think it is possible for a person to develop a phobia of the color red? If yes, why? If no, why not? Support your position either way.

MULTIPLE CHOICE

The following multiple choice questions will test your comprehension of the material presented in the chapter. Circle the correct choice for each question in the section. Then compare your answers with those at the end of the chapter.

1. A diffuse, vague, very unpleasant feeling of fear and dread is characteristics of

   a. a phobia.
   b. anxiety.
   c. motor tension.
   d. hypervigilance.

2. Which of the statements below is not characteristic of a self-description of anxiety?

   a. " My heart thumps often."
   b. " I'm under constant strain."
   c. " I tend to make quick decisions."
   d. " I always seem to be dreading something."

3. Which of the following is not a symptom of generalized anxiety disorder?

   a. motor tension
   b. autonomic reactivity
   c. hypervigilance
   d. sensations of floating

4. The term _____ refers to an abrupt surge of intense anxiety that is cued by a particular stimulus or without obvious cues.

   a. panic attack
   b. obsession
   c. compulsion
   d. hypervigilance

5.　A study by Eaton and others (1994) found that _____ of 8,098 people surveyed reported a panic attack during the course of their lives.

a. 3%
b. 10%
c. 15%
d. 27%

6.　All of the following statements are true of panic disorders except

a. They tend to run in families.
b. They are usually associated with childhood trauma.
c. The person may also experience other types of maladaptive behavior.
d. Severe panic reactions may be followed by psychotic disorganization.

7.　Marks (1987) believes that panic and anticipatory anxiety

a. are essentially the same.
b. should both be treated with antidepressants.
c. are not valid DSM categories.
d. have different sources.

8.　The majority of patients with panic disorder experience _____ , while most patients with generalized anxiety disorder experience

a. muscular weakness; sweating.
b. blurred vision; faintness.
c. heart palpitations; heart palpitations.
d. sweating; chest pain.

9.　Of the following, which is true of panic disorders?

a. It is the most common form of anxiety disorder.
b. It affects more men than women.
c. It is more frequently found in younger people than in older individuals.
d. It does not run in families.

10.　Which of the following is not one of the general types of phobias?

a. agoraphobia
b. claustrophobia
c. specific
d. social

11. The most common type of phobia is

   a. fear of heights.
   b. fear of water.
   c. fear of open spaces.
   d. fear of closed spaces.

12. Phobics

   a. must be presented with the feared stimulus in order to become anxious.
   b. spend considerable energy avoiding the feared stimulus.
   c. tend to be predominately male.
   d. both a & c.

13. Select the following category which is not typical of phobias.

   a. mutilation fears
   b. animal fears
   c. nature fears
   d. intimacy fears

14. _____ is characterized by fear and embarrassment in dealings with other people.

   a. Simple phobia
   b. Social phobia
   c. Xenophobia
   d. Claustrophobia

15. The fears of _____ and _____ are particularly resistant types of social phobias.

   a. blushing; eating
   b. dating; eating
   c. blushing; dating
   d. blushing; public speaking

16. If a patient has a social phobia, a self-help technique they can use effectively is

   a. avoid eye contact.
   b. fill silences in conversation.
   c. initiate conversation.
   d. set limits on a person who attempts to criticize them.

17. An agoraphobic's fear centers on

   a. bugs.
   b. losing control in a crowd.
   c. water.
   d. heights.

18. A patient comes to treatment complaining of an "irresistible urge" to make sure that every window in her apartment is locked before leaving for work. The patient further confides that she will often check and recheck the windows before leaving the apartment. Thus, she is often late for work. This patient would be diagnosed as suffering from

   a. a phobia regarding unlocked windows.
   b. low motivation for arriving to work on time.
   c. a compulsion.
   d. none of the above.

19. _____ usually involve doubt, hesitation, fear of contamination, or fear of one's own aggression.

   a. Obsessions
   b. Compulsions
   c. Phobias
   d. Neuroses

20. Behavior rituals that the person feels compelled to perform are called

   a. obsessions.
   b. compulsions.
   c. phobias.
   d. neuroses

21. Choose the statement below that is true of obsessive-compulsive disorders.

   a. Patients tend to be secretive about their preoccupations.
   b. It is more common in lower income individuals.
   c. The disorder begins in early childhood.
   d. In general, patients tend to be married.

22. Which of the following is not one of the four types of preoccupations common among obsessive-compulsive individuals?

   a. checking rituals
   b. cleaning rituals

c. slowness
d. ignoring details

23. From the psychodynamic view, the major determinants of anxiety disorders are

a. conditioned responses.
b. inappropriate patterns of reinforcement.
c. unconscious motivations.
d. irrational beliefs.

24. The case in the text which discusses "special routines" for getting dressed in the morning is illustrative of

a. a social phobia.
b. the development of a compulsion.
c. agoraphobia.
d. a social compulsion.

25. Sherry is obsessed with her husband's welfare and calls him four times a day at the office. She has admitted to her family that she resents the amount of time her husband spends at work. In psychodynamic terms, this woman is probably using _____ as a defense mechanism.

a. rationalization
b. projection
c. intellectualization
d. reaction formation

26. Which of the following is not part of the behavioral approach to treating anxiety disorders?

a. systematic desensitization
b. modeling
c. flooding
d. isolation

27. In _____ a series of fear-arousing stimuli, carefully graded from mild to strongly fearful, are very gradually introduced to the client.

a. implosive therapy
b. systematic desensitization
c. modeling
d. flooding

28. The cognitive perspective on anxiety disorders emphasizes

   a. unconscious motivations.
   b. unrealistic evaluations of situations.
   c. the symbolic significance of behaviors.
   d. reaction formation and isolation.

29. Cognitive restructuring helps clients to

   a. understand childhood fears.
   b. gradually learn to approach a feared object.
   c. mentally rehearse adaptive responses.
   d. develop more realistic evaluations of situations.

30. Loudly saying "stop" is a component of

   a. systematic desensitization
   b. cognitive restructuring
   c. thought stopping
   d. modeling

31. Which of the following is not one of the side effects of benzodiazepines?

   a. drowsiness
   b. reduced ability to concentrate
   c. hyperactivity
   d. confusion

32. A study by Spiegel and others (1994) demonstrated that _____ was especially effective in treating panic disorders.

   a. Alprozolam
   b. cognitive-behavioral treatment
   c. Alprozolam and cognitive-behavioral treatment
   d. none of the above

TRUE/FALSE QUESTIONS

Indicate whether each statement is true or false. Check your answers at the end of this chapter.

1.   There seems to be growing evidence that over-sensitivity to threat cues is a significant problem for individuals with anxiety disorders.

2.   The experience of anxiety is always maladaptive.

3.   People who suffer from anxiety disorders are very much aware of the reasons for their fears.

4.   Panic attacks can range in time from several minutes to several hours.

5.   Over 50% of patients with panic attacks have attempted suicide.

6.   Persons who experience panic attacks tend to be frequent users of emergency rooms.

7.   Phobic persons seldom develop ways of reducing their fears.

8.   Stimuli that initiate phobias tend to be random.

9.   Xenophobia is a fear of flying.

10.   Fifty percent of people who have panic disorders develop agoraphobia.

11.   Compulsive rituals may become very elaborate.

12.   The exact prevalence of obsessive-compulsive disorder is well known.

13.   Implosive therapy places an individual in direct contact with a feared stimulus.

14.   Thought stopping is essentially a self-control technique.

MATCHING

Match the following terms with information provided below. Check your answers at the end of this chapter.

a.   implosive therapy
b.   reaction formation
c.   obsession
d.   in vivo exposure
e.   social phobia

f.   hypervigilance
g.   comorbidity
h.   specific phobia
i.   compulsion
j.   "sense of strangeness"

_____ overlap of symptoms among patients with different disorders
_____ feature of a panic attack
_____ repetitive thoughts
_____ presentation of actual feared stimulus
_____ fear and embarrassment in dealing with others
_____ symptom of generalized anxiety disorder
_____ includes fear of animals
_____ repetitive actions
_____ behaving in a manner opposite underlying feelings
_____ imagined recreation of fear-arousing situation

ANSWER KEY

Multiple Choice

1. B	17. B
2. C	18. C
3. D	19. A
4. A	20. B
5. A	21. A
6. B	22. D
7. D	23. C
8. C	24. B
9. C	25. D
10. B	26. D
11. A	27. B
12. B	28. B
13. D	29. D
14. B	30. C
15. A	31. C
16. C	32. B

True/False

1. T
2. F
3. F
4. T
5. F
6. T
7. F

8. F
9. F
10. T
11. T
12. F
13. F

Matching

g
j
c
d
e
f
h
i
b
a

Chapter 8
SEXUAL VARIATIONS AND DISORDERS

CHAPTER OVERVIEW

This chapter considers two types of sexual behaviors: those that are often personally problematic (sexual dysfunctions) and those that differ from the norms of society (paraphilias). Historical perspectives on sexuality are traced and theories as well as research findings and treatment modalities are discussed. Contemporary views on homosexuality and bisexuality, which are no longer considered to be psychological disorders, are reviewed. Finally, the types and rates of sexual victimization, and the approaches to their treaments are explored.

CHAPTER OUTLINE

Changing Views of Sexual Behavior

Surveys of Sexual Behavior

Homosexuality
       Attitudes Toward Homosexuality
       Origins of Sexual Orientation

Sexual Dysfunction
       Types of Sexual Dysfunction
       Treatment of Sexual Dysfunction
       The Effectiveness of Sex Therapy

Gender Identity Disorder
       Gender Identity Problems in Childhood
       Gender Identity Disorder in Adults

The Paraphilias
       Fetishism
       Transvestic Fetishism
       Sexual Sadism and Masochism
       Voyeurism
       Exhibitionism
       Pedophilia
       Perspectives on the Paraphilias

Sexual Victimization
    Rape
    Child Sexual Abuse

LEARNING OBJECTIVES

You should know:

1.   cultural and historical bases of attitudes toward sex.

2.   findings and impact of the Kinsey surveys.

3.   how sexual orientation develops and is viewed.

4.   the research findings on the psychological adjustment of homosexuals and their relationship patterns.

5.   the distinguishing traits of bisexuality and its effects on relationships.

6.   the major types of sexual dysfunctions of both men and women and the treatment approaches for them.

7.   the characteristics of gender identity problems from mild forms to transsexualism.

8.   the varieties of paraphilias and treatments for them.

9.   the categories of rape and characteristics associated with being a rapist.

10.   the incidence and circumstances surrounding child sexual abuse and incest.

KEY TERMS AND CONCEPTS

Following is a list of key terms and concepts that are featured in the chapter and are important for you to know. Write out the definitions of each of these terms and check your answers with the definitions in the text.

homosexual behavior
homosexual
lesbian
bisexual
sexual dysfunction
erectile dysfunction
inhibited sexual excitement
nocturnal penile tumescence
performance anxiety
premature ejaculation
retarded ejaculation
anorgasmia
dyspareunia
vaginismus
sensate focus
gender identity
gender identity disorder of childhood
transsexualism
nontranssexual gender identity disorder
paraphilia
fetishism
transvestism
sadist
masochist
voyeurism
exhibitionist
pedophilia
sex offenders
rape
power rape
anger rape
sadistic rape

CRITICAL THINKING QUESTIONS

In developing answers for the following questions, turn to the section of your chapter that covers the pertinent material. Read the section thoroughly before attempting to frame your answer.

1. What do recent surveys reveal regarding the changing views of sexual behavior in the U.S.?

2. How have our attitudes toward homosexuality changed? What is bisexuality?

3. What is a sexual dysfunction? List the types presented in your text and briefly explain them.

4. How are sexual dysfunctions treated? Describe the Masters and Johnson approach.

5. Explain the behavioral and cognitive approaches to treating sexual dysfunction.

6. Overall, how effective is sex therapy?

7. Discuss the nature of gender identity disorders.

8. Provide a definition for paraphilias. List and discuss the types presented in your text.

9. How do the various theories attempt to explain paraphilia?

10. Review the research on rape, child sexual abuse and incest. What population is at high risk for sexual abuse?

11. In your opinion, is child sexual abuse on the rise? If so, what factors may play a role in the increase?

MULTIPLE CHOICE

The following multiple choice questions will test your comprehension of the material presented in the chapter. Circle the correct choice for each question in the section. Then compare your answers with those at the end of the chapter.

1. Select the following statement which is not true of Kinsey's research?

   a. It was the first major study of sexual practices in the U.S.
   b. There was a volunteer bias in his sample.
   c. In-depth interviews were used to collect data.
   d. He found that sexual dysfunction could not be treated successfully.

2. Laumann and others' (1994) study through the National Opinion Research Center found

    a. the median number of sexual partners for a man is 10.
    b. monogamous couples have the most sex and are the happiest.
    c. 10% of men report having a sexual encounter with a male in adulthood.
    d. both a & b.

3. It appears that teenagers have sex for the first time because of

    a. affection.
    b. affection and peer pressure.
    c. peer pressure.
    d. none of the above.

4. Which of the following is not a change in social customs found in a recent survey?

    a. There has been an increase in cohabitation before marriage.
    b. There is an increase in rates of divorce and remarriage.
    c. Nontraditional types of sexual relationships are accepted more.
    d. Oral sex is still perceived to be perverted.

5. What percentage of men find group sex very appealing?

    a. 52
    b. 14
    c. 3
    d. 20

6. Choose the statement below that is true of homosexuals.

    a. A person's belief about homosexuality is dependent upon actual behavior.
    b. The term "homosexual" is preferred over the term "gay".
    c. Someone with no sexual experience usually thinks of himself/herself as heterosexual.
    d. Many homosexuals have heterosexual fantasies.

7. According to a recent public opinion poll, _____ % of American respondents said they believe homosexual relationships are morally wrong.

    a. 10
    b. 57
    c. 44
    d. none of the above

8.   Both the American Psychological Association and the American Psychiatric Association

a. have retained homosexuality as a psychiatric disorder.
b. have found that homosexuals differ in their psychological adjustment from heterosexuals.
c. do not consider homosexuality to be a mental illness.
d. consider bisexuality to be a psychiatric disorder.

9.   LeVay (1991) found

a. no difference in the anatomical structure of the hypothalamus between gay and heterosexual men.
b. a difference in the form of the hypothalamus between gay men and heterosexual men.
c. a difference in the level of psychological adjustment between homosexual and heterosexual men.
d. both a & c.

10.   A potential confounding factor in the above study was

a. the age of the subjects.
b. coronary heart disease.
c. AIDS.
d. the sexual orientation of the subjects.

11.   The rate of bisexuality in the U.S.

a. is difficult to estimate.
b. has decreased over the last several years.
c. is increasing as a function of changing attitudes.
d. is estimated to be 29%.

12.   A sexual dysfunction

a. refers to an impairment of an organic nature.
b. refers to an impairment in sexual response.
c. refers to an impairment of sexual interest.
d. both b & c.

13. Which of the following factors has not been identified as a cause of sexual dysfunction?

    a. infidelity
    b. number of children
    c. alcohol
    d. fatigue

14. Choose the following statement that has not been identified as a psychological correlate of sexual dysfunction.

    a. fear of rejection
    b. inhibitions about nakedness
    c. difficulty expressing tender emotions
    d. need for achievement

15. Select the accurate order of the sexual response cycle.

    a. appetitive, excitement, orgasm, resolution
    b. orgasm, excitement, appetitive, resolution
    c. excitement, appetitive, orgasm, resolution
    d. appetitive, orgasm, excitement, resolution

16. Erectile dysfunction occurs during the _____ stage of the sexual-response cycle.

    a. excitement
    b. appetitive
    c. resolution
    d. orgasm

17. Identify the statement below that is true of the relationship between sexual dysfunction and the marital relationship.

    a. Sexual problems are only found in the context of a dysfunctional relationship.
    b. Most of the time, sexual problems indicate a problem in the relationship.
    c. Sexual problems can occur in a well functioning marriage.
    d. None of the above.

18. _____ is a disorder of the orgasm phase in females.

    a. Vaginismus
    b. Inorgasmia
    c. Dyspareunia
    d. Anorgasmia

19.   _____ refers to genital pain before, during, or after intercourse.

   a. Vaginismus
   b. Anorgasmia
   c. Dyspareunia
   d. Retarded dysparia

20.   LoPiccolo (1994) states that modern sex therapy is a combination of family systems therapy, cognitive and behavioral techniques and

   a. Psychodynamic approaches.
   b. Rational emotive approaches.
   c. Operant conditioning approaches.
   d. Systematic desensitization.

21.   Which of the following is not a general goal for couples in sex therapy?

   a. mutual communication
   b. decreasing the fears of failure
   c. shifting attention to the experience of pleasure
   d. increase the rate of orgasms of both partners

22.   A couple experiencing a sexual dysfunction is in the early stages of learning Masters and Johnson's sensate focusing techniques. They have most likely been told to

   a. attempt to have sexual intercourse several times a day.
   b. pretend that each person is making love to a "fantasy partner" such as a movie star.
   c. caress and explore the partner's body without attempting sexual intercourse.
   d. analyze the roots of the sexual problem that occurred during early childhood experiences.

23.   The case of the 24-year-old lawyer who had an inability to retain an erection is illustrative of

   a. the psychoanalytic approach to treating sexual disorders.
   b. the use of a cognitive behavioral approach to treating sexual dysfunction.
   c. the use of biofeedback in treating sexual dysfunction.
   d. the failure of the Kaplan approach.

24. Success rates for sex therapy are reported to range from

a. 39% to 98%.
b. 5% to 31%.
c. 98% to 99%.
d. 39% to 89%.

25. Gender identity refers to a person's

a. sexual preference.
b. genetic composition.
c. feeling of being male or female.
d. male or female genital organs.

26. Sexual preference is synonymous with

a. sexual orientation.
b. one's preference for type of sexual activity.
c. a preference for certain characteristics with a given sex.
d. both a & c.

27. A young girl refuses to wear dresses and states, " I'm a boy. Boys wear pants."
This child would probably be described as exhibiting

a. childhood homosexuality.
b. transgender identity conflict.
c. a gender identity disorder of childhood.
d. a nontranssexual gender identity disorder of childhood.

28. People who have a very intense desire to change their sexual status, including their
anatomical structures, are called

a. homosexuals.
b. transvestites.
c. paraphilias.
d. transsexuals.

29. According to Lindemalm and others (1986), what fraction of cases of male-to-
female transsexuals experience fair to good sexual adjustment?

a. 1/2
b. 1/8
c. 2/3
d. 1/3

30. Which of the following is not a paraphilia?

    a. fetishism
    b. transvestism
    c. sadism
    d. homosexuality

31. In a _____, a non-living object serves as the primary source of sexual arousal and consummation.

    a. parataxia
    b. dysparneuia
    c. fetish
    d. parafetish

32. Select the statement below that is true.

    a. Fetishism usually begins in early adulthood.
    b. Most fetishists are female.
    c. In some cases, crimes are committed to obtain the desired object.
    d. Fetishists prefer to experience arousal in the presence of others.

33. Bill becomes sexually aroused by dressing in women's lingerie. His behavior is characteristic of

    a. transsexualism.
    b. transvestism.
    c. a gender identity disorder.
    d. masochism.

34. Covert sensitization involves

    a. replacing aversive imagery.
    b. pleasurable imagery with aversive imagery.
    c. avoiding anxiety-producing imagery.
    d. both a & c.

35. The five features most commonly found in cases of sadomasochism include agreement on dominant and submissive roles, awareness of role playing, a sexual context, a shared understanding of sadomasochism, and

    a. a history of early childhood abuse.
    b. a desire to become the opposite sex.
    c. the consent of both partners.
    d. inhibited sexual desire.

36. Which of the following is not true about individuals who engage in voyeurism or exhibitionism?

    a. It is a compulsive behavior.
    b. They are almost always male.
    c. They are usually harmless.
    d. Most individuals are married.

37. The psychodynamic perspective views paraphilic behavior to be a function of

    a. learning.
    b. modeling the same-sex parent.
    c. unresolved conflicts.
    d. a fixation of the superego.

38. Rape is

    a. a form of paraphilia.
    b. divided into three types.
    c. an under reported crime.
    d. b and c.

39. A criticism of the use of dolls in investigating child sexual abuse is that

    a. they are not life-like enough.
    b. they are overly suggestive.
    c. children do not relate well to them.
    d. the dolls are too threatening.

40. Which of the following is not a consequence for rape survivors?

    a. loss of self esteem
    b. loss of weight
    c. social phobia
    d. obsessive-compulsive disorder

41. Incest differs from pedophilia in that

    a. it is a crime.
    b. it is committed by strangers.
    c. it refers to contact between biologically related individuals.
    d. it causes no psychological problems in victims.

TRUE/FALSE QUESTIONS

Indicate whether each statement is true or false. Check your answers at the end of this chapter.

1. The early Greeks regarded sex with partners of either sex as normal.

2. Many homosexuals have heterosexual fantasies.

3. Geography plays a role in the formation of homosexual communities.

4. Homosexuality between women is called lesbianism.

5. Denmark allows homosexuals to marry.

6. Homosexuals differ in psychological adjustment from heterosexuals.

7. It appears that sexual orientation is due to a multitude of factors.

8. If a sexual problem is due entirely to organic factors, it is termed a sexual dysfunction.

9. Performance anxiety is not a contributing factor to impotence.

10. In treating sexual dysfunctions, Masters and Johnson emphasize communication between partners.

11. Sexual fantasies are considered maladaptive.

12. Transsexual surgery remains controversial.

13. Fetishism is one of the most puzzling forms of sexual behavior.

14. Only women are considered to be transvestites.

15. Sadomasochists may be heterosexual, bisexual or homosexual.

16. No one type of treatment is superior in treating paraphilias.

17. Children in step, foster and adoptive families have a high risk for sexual abuse.

MATCHING

Match the following terms with information provided below. The answers may be found at the end of the chapter.

a.   gender identity
b.   nocturnal penile tumescence
c.   fetishism
d.   sensate focus
e.   masochist

f.   erectile dysfunction
g.   power rape
h.   paraphilia
i.   transvestism
j.   anorgasmia

_____ sexual satisfaction is based on pain/humiliation
_____ inability to attain or hold an erection
_____ inability to achieve orgasm in women
_____ means "attraction to the deviant"
_____ changes in penis during sleep
_____ sexual-retraining technique
_____ refers to person's feeling of being male or female
_____ use of non-living object as source of sexual arousal and consummation
_____ cross-dressing
_____ victim is threatened with physical harm

ANSWER KEY

Multiple Choice

1. b	20. a
2. b	21. d
3. b	22. c
4. d	23. b
5. b	24. a
6. d	25. c
7. d	26. a
8. c	27. c
9. b	28. d
10. c	29. d
11. a	30. d
12. d	31. c
13. b	32. c
14. d	33. b
15. a	34. b
16. a	35. c
17. c	36. d
18. d	37. c
19. c	38. d

39. b
40. b

41. c

True/False

1. T
2. T
3. T
4. T
5. T
6. F
7. T
8. F
9. F

10. T
11. F
12. T
13. T
14. F
15. T
16. T
17. T

Matching
e
f
j
h
b
d
a
c
i
g

Chapter 9
PERSONALITY DISORDERS

CHAPTER OVERVIEW

Personality disorders are considered to be long-standing, maladaptive patterns of behavior. A primary characteristic of this type of disorder is "inflexibility". In this section, the major types of personality disorders are presented in three broad categories: odd/eccentric, dramatic/emotional/erratic, and anxious/fearful. The chapter also discusses associated diagnostic criteria, relevant theory, and obstacles to classification.

CHAPTER OUTLINE

Classifying Personality Disorders

Odd or Eccentric Behaviors
      Paranoid Personality Disorder
      Schizoid Personality Disorder
      Schizotypal Personality Disorder

Dramatic, Emotional, or Erratic Behaviors
      Histrionic Personality Disorder
      Narcissistic Personality Disorder
      Borderline Personality Disorder
      Antisocial Personality Disorder

Anxious or Fearful Behaviors
      Avoidant Personality Disorder
      Dependent Personality Disorder
      Obsessive-Compulsive Personality Disorder

Treatment of Personality Disorders

The Outlook for Personality Disorder Classification

LEARNING OBJECTIVES

You should know:

1. what a personality disorder is and how it relates to a person's personality.

2. that the characteristic behaviors of personality disorders are episodic and dependent on the influence of different situations.

3. how personality disorders are classified according to DSM-IV, the difficulties involved in making these diagnoses, and the future prospects for classifying them.

4. how the diagnosis of personality disorders on Axis II meshes with the primary diagnosis on Axis I.

5. the major clinical features of each of the personality disorders discussed in the chapter.

6. how borderline personality disorders are distinguished from other personality disorders and the hypotheses as to their cause.

7. the research results on the possible causes of antisocial personality disorders and the difficulties of the antisocial personality disorder diagnostic criteria.

8. the differences between obsessive-compulsive anxiety disorders, and obsessive-compulsive personality disorder.

9. some of the reasons for the relatively limited knowledge of personality disorders.

10. the methods used to treat personality disorders and their effectiveness.

KEY TERMS AND CONCEPTS

Following is a list of key terms and concepts that are featured in the chapter and are important for you to know. Write out the definitions of each of these terms and check your answers with the definitions in the text.

personality
personality disorders
symptom disorders
prototypal approach
paranoid personality disorder
schizoid personality disorder

schizotypal personality disorder
histrionic personality disorder
narcissistic personality disorder
borderline personality disorder
splitting
antisocial personality disorder
avoidant personality disorder
dependent personality disorder
obsessive-compulsive personality disorder
categorical model
dimensional model

CRITICAL THINKING QUESTIONS

In developing answers for the following questions, turn to the section of your chapter that covers the pertinent material. Read the section thoroughly before attempting to frame your answer.

1.   What are the characteristic behaviors of personality disorders?

2.   Why do the personality disorders present problems in classification?

3.   What is the prototypal approach of DSM-IV?

4.   Describe the characteristics associated with paranoid personality disorders.

5.   What symptoms might be expected of a schizoid personality disorder?

6.   List characteristics associated with the schizotypal personality disorder.

7.   Histrionic personality disorders display what symptoms?

8.   Describe the symptoms associated with narcissistic personality disorder.

9.   What kind of behaviors might one expect of a borderline personality disorder? Recent research suggests three distinctive features of this disorder. What are they?

10.   The term "psychopath" is often used to describe people who exhibit traits of an antisocial personality disorder. What are these traits? Research on this personality disorder has proven to be interesting. What are the current research findings?

11.   List the traits of an avoidant personality disorder.

12. Explain the prominent features in dependent personality disorder.

13. An individual who is diagnosed as having an obsessive-personality disorder presents what behaviors?

14. What are the additional proposed categories of personality disorders and why are they controversial?

15. Why is the treatment of the personality disorders difficult and seldom successful?

MULTIPLE CHOICE

The following multiple choice questions will test your comprehension of the material presented in the chapter. Circle the correct choice for each question, then compare your answers with those at the end of the chapter.

1. Which of the following statements is false regarding personality disorders?

   a. They are longstanding, maladaptive ways of dealing with the environment.
   b. They are usually noticed in childhood or in early adolescence.
   c. They allow for only a rigid and narrow range of responses to situations.
   d. They are estimated to occur in 49% of the population.

2. Select the statement below that is correct.

   a. Little is known about the origins and development of a personality disorder.
   b. Personality disorders are severely incapacitating.
   c. Much research exists on the nature of personality disorders.
   d. They are diagnosed on Axis I.

3. The major personality disorders may be divided into three groups: odd/eccentric, dramatic/emotional, and

   a. sadistic/avoidant.
   b. aggressive/fearful.
   c. anxious/fearful.
   d. seductive/sexual.

4. Jim exhibits feelings of suspiciousness, hypersensitivity, and mistrust of his coworkers. He is perceived as "cold" by them. Typically, these types of traits are seen in

    a. paranoid personality disorders.
    b. schizoid personality disorders.
    c. schizophrenia.
    d. prototypal personality disorders.

5. Margo works as a night receptionist in a high rise apartment building. She is viewed by tenants as "weird and aloof" because she never acknowledges them unless spoken to first. She is unmarried and lives alone in the apartment building and does not appear to socialize or date. Margo appears to exhibit characteristics of a _____ disorder.

    a. schizotypal
    b. schizoid
    c. atypical personality
    d. antisocial

6. A schizotypal personality disorder is characterized by

    a. a break from reality.
    b. attention-seeking.
    c. intense emotional attachments.
    d. oddities of speech.

7. Jean is an overly dramatic person. She is seen by others as being vain and immature. Because of her self-centered attitude and manipulative behaviors, relationships with others tend to be stormy. She first came to the attention of a therapist because of a superficial and dramatic attempt to commit suicide by taking an almost toxic dose of vitamins. The therapist would likely diagnose Jean as a

    a. paranoid personality disorder.
    b. schizotypal personality disorder.
    c. narcissistic personality disorder.
    d. histrionic personality disorder.

8. Mary is engaged to marry Joe but has concerns about some things. For example, Joe is very intolerant of others and often seems to require excessive admiration and attention. Given this information, select a tentative diagnosis for Joe.

    a. narcissistic personality disorder
    b. histrionic personality disorder

c. schizotypal personality disorder

d. none of the above

9.   A therapist who is treating a client who is diagnosed as a borderline personality disorder should expect which of the following to occur?

a. The client is likely to ask for special favors, and will try to impress the therapist with his brilliance.

b. Self-destructive behaviors designed to call forth a "saving" response from the therapist have a high probability of occurring.

c. The thinking of the client is likely to deteriorate under stress and the client might express some delusional thoughts.

d. A pattern of irresponsible behaviors, lack of conscience, and lying will probably characterize this client's behavior.

10.   According to Kernberg, the borderline personality disorder is characterized by a failure to integrate the positive and negative experiences that occur between the individual and other people--a phenomenon known as

a. autism.

b. egocentric behavior.

c. egotistical behavior.

d. splitting.

11.   Which of the following is not a problem in cases of borderline personality disorder?

a. affective disturbances

b. impulse disturbances

c. reality disturbances

d. identity disturbances

12.   Choose the following statement that is not true of Linehan's (1993) dialectical behavior therapy for borderline personality disorder.

a. It combines cognitive, behavioral and psychodynamic concepts.

b. It is aimed particularly at suicidal threats and gestures.

c. It uses individual and group therapy.

d. It emphasizes that patients become independent of others.

13.   The case of Gary Gilmore illustrates many symptoms of

a. a conduct disorder.

b. an antisocial personality disorder.

c. a borderline personality disorder.

d. a narcissistic personality disorder.

14. According to Gottesman and Goldsmith (1994),

    a. learning theory presents the best explanation of how antisocial personality develops.
    b. heredity may play a role in criminality and antisocial behavior.
    c. brain wave patterns have failed to show significance in the study of antisocial personality disorder.
    d. none of the above.

15. From a cognitive perspective, the study of antisocial behavior focuses on

    a. moral development.
    b. patterns of brain wave activity.
    c. differing levels of neurotransmitters.
    d. left-handedness and right-brain dominance.

16. Select the following statement that is true.

    a. Abused children are at greater risk for being diagnosed as antisocial personality disorder in adulthood.
    b. There is no relationship between abuse in childhood and antisocial personality disorder in adulthood.
    c. People diagnosed as having antisocial personality disorder do not report being abused in childhood.
    d. Both b and c.

17. A person with an avoidant personality disorder experiences conflict over

    a. desires to be good and impulses toward hostile and violent behavior.
    b. wanting affection and doubting their acceptance by others.
    c. fears of looking foolish and wanting to be the center of attention.
    d. obsessions about germs or dirt and inability to maintain a totally clean environment.

18. _____ personality disorders tend to be "clinging" according to Bornstein (1992).

    a. Avoidant
    b. Narcissistic
    c. Antisocial
    d. Dependent

19. An individual with a dependent personality disorder believes that

   a. he/she deserves the best.
   b. he/she is more important than others.
   c. others are dependent on him/her.
   d. he/she must act meek and obedient to keep another's attention.

20. Morgan describes his friend Dylan as somewhat "stiff and formal". Dylan's rigid perfectionism and morality often drives Morgan over the edge. However, since Dylan has been eccentric since he was a young boy, Morgan tries to overlook Dylan's quirks. Which of the following would most likely apply to Dylan?

   a. obsessive-compulsive personality disorder
   b. obsessive-compulsive anxiety disorder
   c. dependent personality disorder
   d. none of the above

21. Read the following statement and match it with its appropriate diagnosis.
   "I must save money. That's why I tend to save things and people call me a packrat."

   a. paranoid personality disorder
   b. obsessive-compulsive personality disorder
   c. dependent personality disorder
   d. schizoid personality disorder

22. Which of the following is not a problem related to a lack of knowledge regarding personality disorders?

   a. People with personality disorders are satisfied with their behavior.
   b. Professionals tend to see a restricted sample of people with these disorders.
   c. They view the environment as the source of their problems.
   d. DSM-IV lacks specific criteria for diagnosis.

23. _____ therapy has been used effectively with personality disorders in which anxious or fearful behavior plays a prominent role.

   a. Behavior
   b. Psychodynamic
   c. Drug
   d. Relaxation

24.   _____ therapy may be a useful part of the treatment of many individuals with personality disorders.

   a. Group
   b. Family
   c. Reality
   d. Both a & b

25.   Some clinicians argue that _____ should be included as a category in DSM-IV personality disorders.

   a. a sadistic pattern
   b. a manic pattern
   c. an ego-maniacal pattern
   d. an argumentative pattern

26.   Axis II of DSM-IV uses a(n) _____ model for classification.

   a. categorical
   b. dimensional
   c. nosological
   d. ICD

TRUE/FALSE QUESTIONS

Indicate whether each statement is true or false. Check your answers at the end of this chapter.

1.   Personality disorders are classified on Axis I of the DSM.

2.   Little is known about the origins of personality disorders.

3.   Personality disorders are often called symptom disorders.

4.   Personality disorders produce the most reliable diagnoses of any DSM disorder.

5.   A person may have a diagnosis on Axis I and Axis II.

6.   Schizoid individuals have a poor prognosis for treatment.

7.   "All the world is a stage" best describes the schizotypal personality disorder.

8. Devaluing the importance of others is characteristic of the borderline personality disorder.

9. "Splitting" refers to the failure to integrate positive and negative aspects of experience.

10. Men are more likely than women to be diagnosed as having histrionic personality disorder.

11. Borderline personality disorders occur in 10% of the general population.

12. Recently, bulimia has become a destructive tactic for borderlines.

13. Individuals with obsessive-compulsive personality disorder are quite good at seeing the "big picture."

14. People with personality disorders frequently seek professional help.

15. Research demonstrates that drug therapy is the best method of treatment for personality disorders.

MATCHING

Match the following terms with information provided below. The answers may be found at the end of the chapter.

a. narcissistic personality disorder
b. borderline personality disorder
c. schizoid personality disorder
d. impulse disturbance
e. personality

f. categorical model
g. prototypal approach
h. dimensional model
i. splitting
j. DIN

_____ shifting between contradictory images
_____ characteristic ways of behaving
_____ classification system used in DSM IV
_____ few, if any, activities provide pleasure
_____ may fantasize about unlimited success
_____ suggests marginal level of functioning
_____ characterized by self-damaging acts
_____ research instrument used to study narcissistic personality disorder
_____ approaches classification through a threshold model
_____ focuses on patterns of personality characteristics

ANSWER KEY

Multiple Choice

1. d
2. a
3. c
4. a
5. b
6. d
7. d
8. a
9. b
10. d
11. c
12. d
13. b

14. b
15. a
16. a
17. b
18. d
19. d
20. a
21. b
22. d
23. b
24. d
25. a
26. a

True/False

1. F
2. T
3. F
4. F
5. T
6. T
7. F
8. T

9. T
10. F
11. F
12. T
13. F
14. F
15. F

Matching

i
e
g
c
a
b
d
j
f
h

Chapter 10
MOOD DISORDERS

CHAPTER OVERVIEW

Mood disorders, characterized by a disturbance in mood or emotion are the topic of interest in this section. The chapter explains depression as a mood state and as a disorder, and presents risk factors identified through research. Topics covered include dysthymic disorder, major depressive disorder, cyclothymic disorder, and bipolar I and II disorders. The chapter gives an extensive overview to treatments of these disorders and information on factors related to suicide.

CHAPTER OUTLINE

Mood Disorders
>   How Common Are Mood Disorders?

Depression
>   Depressed Mood
>   Risk Factors
>   Life Events

Depressive Disorders
>   Dysthymic Disorder
>   Major Depressive Disorder

Theoretical Perspectives on Depression
>   Biological Theories
>   The Psychodynamic View
>   The Behavioral Perspective
>   The Cognitive Perspective
>   The Humanistic-Existential Perspective
>   Depression from a Vulnerability-Resilience Perspective

Treatment of Depression
>   Biologically Based Treatment
>   Behavioral Treatment for Depression
>   Cognitive Therapy for Depression
>   Contrasting Psychological Therapies for Depression
>   Effectiveness of Biological and Psychological Therapies for Depression

The Bipolar Disorders
    Cyclothymic Disorder
    Bipolar I Disorder
    Bipolar II Disorder
    The Course of Bipolar Disorder
    Causes of Bipolar Disorder
    Treatment of Bipolar Disorder

Suicide
    Risk Factors
    Hopelessness
    Attitudes Toward Suicide
    The Impact of Suicide on Others

LEARNING OBJECTIVES

You should know:

1. the epidemiological findings on the rates of mood disorders in the United States.

2. the risk factors for having depression.

3. the defining characteristics of dysthymia.

4. what the signs of major depression are.

5. the biological theories of the etiology of depression, including the kinds of drugs available; and ECT, including its advantages and disadvantages.

6. the biological treatments for depression; drug therapy, including the kinds of drugs available; and ECT, including its advantages and disadvantages.

7. psychodynamic, behavioral, cognitive, and humanistic-existential theories of depression and the interactional view that derives from them.

8. the defining characteristics of manic and hypomanic episodes and the role played by heredity in their occurance.

9. the role of bipolar disorder in artistic creativity.

10. causes of suicide and its impact on others.

KEY TERMS AND CONCEPTS

Following is a list of key terms and concepts that are featured in the chapter and are important for you to know. Write out the definitions of each of these terms and check your answers with the definitions in the text.

mood disorder
affective disorder
depressive disorder
unipolar disorder
dysthymic disorder
major depressive episode
major depressive episode
monoamine neurotransmitters
catecholomines
indolamine
gamma aminobutyric acid
acetylcholine
vesicles
synaptic clef
catecholamine theory
dexamethasone suppression test
seasonal affective disorder
monoamine oxidase inhibitors
second generation antidepressants
heterocyclics
electroconvulsive therapy
interpersonal psychotherapy
schemas
social skills training
cognitive triad
learned helplessness
hopelessness depression
tricyclics
selective serotonin reuptake inhibitors
cognitive-behavior therapy
cyclothymic disorder
mania
hypomanic episode
bipolar I disorder
bipolar II disorder
postvention

CRITICAL THINKING QUESTIONS

In developing answers for the following questions, turn to the section of your chapter that covers the pertinent material. Read the section thoroughly before attempting to frame your answer.

1. What are the different categories of mood disorders?

2. How can you differentiate between clinical depression and sadness? The term depression can refer to a symptom and to a disorder. Explain this.

3. What are the risk factors for depression?

4. Discuss the contribution of stressful life events to mood disorders.

5. What is a dysthymic disorder? Describe its symptoms.

6. What are the characteristics of a major depression?

7. How do the biological theories explain the origin of a mood disorder? Discuss the research presented throughout the chapter which strongly points to a biological basis for mood disorders. What types of research designs are typically used to assess the biological contributions to mood disorders?

8. What is the dexamethasone suppression test (DST) and what is its effectiveness?

9. Describe the biological treatments used in treating depression. How effective are these interventions?

10. Present the psychodynamic views of depression.

11. How do the behaviorists conceptualize depression?

12. Explain how the cognitive model views and treats depressive disorders. Describe Beck's cognitive-distortion model.

13. Explain the existential-humanistic position on depression.

14. What are the characteristics and causes of a bipolar disorder? Describe the two types discussed in your text. What is mania? What is a cyclothymic disorder?

15. What treatments are available for individuals with bipolar disorders?

16.   What are the risk factors of suicide for persons with mood disorders? Discuss the causes of suicide. Explain the rationale for postvention.

MULTIPLE CHOICE

The following multiple choice questions will test your comprehension of the material presented in the chapter. Circle the correct choice for each question in the section. Then compare your answers with those at the end of the chapter.

1.   The essential feature of a mood disorder is

        a. a delusion.
        b. a disturbance in mood or emotional reaction not due to any other physical or mental disorder.
        c. a manic episode.
        d. parasuicidal behavior.

2.   In the Epidemiological Catchment Area Study (Weissman et al., 1990), _____ percent of the people surveyed met the criteria for a mood disorder one or more times in the past year.

        a. 20.2
        b. 7.8
        c. 4.6
        d. 3.2

3.   After a death, survivors often experience

        a. grief.
        b. the blues.
        c. cyclothymia.
        d. none of the above.

4.   In a National Mental Health Association Poll, _____ percent classified depression as a "personal weakness", while _____ percent categorized it as a "health problem".

        a. 50, 46
        b. 43, 50
        c. 43, 46
        d. 53, 56

5. Which of the following is a risk factor for depression?

   a. heredity
   b. age
   c. gender
   d. all of the above

6. The risk for a first episode of depression is highest in women between the ages of _____ and _____.

   a. 20, 39
   b. 18, 40
   c. 20, 29
   d. 50, 65

7. Which of the following is true regarding the changing rate of major depression?

   a. A person's birth cohort is not a significant predictor of major depression.
   b. There has been an increase in the rate of major depression over time in all countries.
   c. While the birth cohort has changed, there is no associated change in rates for major depression.
   d. Both a & c.

8. Henderson (1992) found which of the findings below in relationship to unsuppportive behaviors and depression?

   a. Unsupportive behaviors can render social support ineffective.
   b. Social support is more important than unsupportive behaviors in buffering the effects of depression.
   c. Unsupportive behavior is not a risk for depression.
   d. Social support and unsupportive behaviors are not directly related to depression.

9. Select the symptom below which is not characteristic of a depressive disorder.

   a. feelings of guilt
   b. loss of interest
   c. difficulty concentrating
   d. impulsive decisions

10.   The term "unipolar" describes

        a. persons who experience mania and depression.
        b. persons who experience depression only.
        c. persons whose grieving is extended.
        d. persons who experience delusions.

11.   The term "dysthymia" means

        a. distorted body image.
        b. different moods.
        c. defective or diseased mood.
        d. chronic mood.

12.   Tim reports feeling tired, sad and experiencing difficulty eating. He also states that
        he derives no enjoyment out of life and that his problems began approximately 4
        years ago. Tim would most probably be diagnosed as having

        a. cyclothymia.
        b. dysthymia.
        c. parasuicidal behavior.
        d. low libido.

13.   The term "double depression" refers to

        a. the presence of dysthymic disorder and major depression, concurrently.
        b. the belief that postpartum depression is twice as high a risk for suicide as
        dysthymia.
        c. the presence of dysthymia in twins.
        d. bipolar II disorders.

14.   In some major depressive episodes, the patient experiences depression and psychotic
        features. An example of this would be

        a. a man who thinks he is the devil.
        b. a woman who thinks she's a sinner.
        c. a woman who thinks she is a goddess.
        d. both a & c

15.   The most widely held view regarding depression is that

        a. it results from an interaction of personal and situational factors.
        b. it is primarily genetic.
        c. it is a learned phenomenon.
        d. situational characteristics are less important than once thought.

16.	Which of the following is not a neurotransmitter which has been associated with depression?

a.	GABA
b.	dopamine
c.	acetycholine
d.	inderamine

17.	Antidepressants work

a.	by increasing the flow of GABA.
b.	by destroying receptor sites.
c.	primarily through producing increased serotonin.
d.	by blocking the ability of MAO to change serotonin into another form.

18.	Dysphoric mood and an inability to experience pleasure appear to be related to

a.	changes in blood flow in the cerebrum.
b.	different metabolic rates within the medulla.
c.	differences in metabolism in the frontal-temporal areas of the cortex.
d.	both a & c

19.	Jones (1994) found that during REM sleep

a.	the serotonin neurons increase in transmission.
b.	the circadian rhythms in the brain cease.
c.	the limbic system suspends functioning.
d.	none of the above.

20.	Which of the following is not a major sleep disturbance found in depression?

a.	shallow sleep
b.	fragmented sleep
c.	short sleep
d.	dream sleep

21.	Freud believed that the depressed patient

a.	lacked adequate superego functioning.
b.	had a punishing superego.
c.	had a rigid ego.
d.	had an insatiable id.

22. _____ has been successfully treated with light therapy.

   a. Hormonal depression
   b. Bipolar depression
   c. Postpartum depression
   d. Seasonal affective disorder

23. A major assumption of interpersonal psychotherapy is

   a. that depression is caused by interpersonal conflict.
   b. that depression is best understood in an interpersonal context.
   c. that drugs are not necessary.
   d. none of the above.

24. Beck's concept of cognitive triad refers to thoughts of

   a. oneself, one's family and the future.
   b. oneself, the situation and the future.
   c. sadness, helplessness and suicide.
   d. sadness, the situation and the future.

25. A person who assumes, "I am the center of everyone's attention, especially of bad performances or personal attributes," is making which of the following cognitive errors according to Beck?

   a. overgeneralizing
   b. selective abstraction
   c. self-references
   d. dichotomous thinking

26. According to Beck's Cognitive-Distortion model

   a. depression is primarily a distortion of mood.
   b. depression is primarily a distortion of thinking.
   c. depression is primarily a distortion of mood and thought.
   d. none of the above.

27. "Cognitive product variables" would include

   a. pessimistic expectations for the future.
   b. self-critical thoughts.
   c. negative self-attributions.
   d. all of the above.

28.   Martin Seligman coined the term

       a. hopelessness depression.
       b. learned helplessness.
       c. suicidal depressive episode.
       d. schemata.

29.   The loss of _____ is the focus of Humanistic-Existential therapists.

       a. self-esteem
       b. the real self
       c. a loved one
       d. hope

30.   A woman in her 40's maintains multiple roles such as wife, mother and employee. If
       this woman were to become depressed, Carl Rogers would assume

       a. she had a genetic predisposition for the disorder.
       b. there was a discrepancy between the ideal and real selves.
       c. she was fixated at the latency stage.
       d. she has depressive schemata.

31.   Which of the following is not a side effect of tricyclics?

       a. rigidity
       b. constipation
       c. dry mouth
       d. ringing in the ears

32.   Select the drug below which is thought to alleviate depression and have an effect on
       personality disorders.

       a. Elavil
       b. Tofranil
       c. Nardil
       d. none of the above

33.   MAO inhibitors have potentially dangerous side effects because

       a. when combined with certain foods they form a toxic substance.
       b. they cause lethargy and have been implicated in auto accidents.
       c. they increase suicidal ideation.
       d. they can lead to psychotic delusions.

34. Select the statement below that is true of ECT.

    a. It is effective for mild to severe depressions.
    b. It results in permanent changes in brain structure.
    c. ECT is rarely used.
    d. ECT treatments prevent recurrence of depression.

35. Choose the option below that accurately identifies the process of cognitive-behavior therapy for depression.

    a. review, agenda, discussion, homework
    b. agenda, discussion, summary, homework
    c. homework, discussion, review, summary
    d. discussion, agenda development, summary, homework

36. The occurrence of _____ is a prerequisite for a diagnosis of bipolar disorder.

    a. delusions of persecution
    b. mania
    c. depression
    d. a sleep disorder

37. A cyclothymic disorder presents as a milder version of

    a. a bipolar I disorder.
    b. a dysthymic disorder.
    c. a bipolar II disorder.
    d. none of the above.

38. Theodore Roosevelt is believed to have been

    a. depressed with psychotic features.
    b. hypomanic.
    c. depressed.
    d. bipolar II.

39. Linda is described as being elated, talkative and hyperactive during the weekend. Her sister recalled that Linda went on a shopping binge and purchased ten purses in the same color. The sister also noted that in a recent conversation, Linda had difficulty staying on a topic. Linda was most probably experiencing a

    a. depressive-anxiety disorder.
    b. hypomanic episode.
    c. depressive episode.
    d. sleep deprivation.

40. In about _____ of the cases where one identical twin has been diagnosed with bipolar disorder, the other twin also received the same diagnosis.

   a. 50%
   b. 10%
   c. 90%
   d. 13%

41. Studies on genetic markers in bipolar disorders have consistently found

   a. a clear Y chromosomal influence.
   b. a direct X chromosomal influence.
   c. no relationship to heredity.
   d. none of the above.

42. The most common treatment of bipolar disorders is

   a. ECT.
   b. lithium.
   c. psychotherapy.
   d. none of the above.

43. Suicide is

   a. the second leading cause of death on college campuses.
   b. not a significant factor in deaths of college students.
   c. on the decrease among high school students.
   d. both b & c.

44. Of the following, which is not a factor associated with suicide in people with mood disorders?

   a. previous suicide attempts.
   b. death of a loved one.
   c. hopelessness.
   d. anxiety.

TRUE/FALSE QUESTIONS

Indicate whether each statement is true or false. Check your answers at the end of this chapter.

1. Almost one out of four hospitalized medical patients has depressive symptoms.

2. Men are twice as likely as women to experience depression.

3. The "pile-up" of stressful life events affects a person's long-term vulnerability to depression.

4. Dysthymic disorder shows little variability with age.

5. Fifty percent of people diagnosed with a major depressive episode will have at least one more episode in their lifetime.

6. Depression is probably the result of a lack of certain chemical neurotransmitters at particular sites in the brain.

7. Beck believes that the tendency to have negative cognitions may have a basis in childhood experiences.

8. Depressed patients are not very realistic about their own social skills.

9. It is believed that President Lincoln experienced bouts of major depression.

10. Antidepressants are the drugs most commonly involved in prescription overdose.

11. ECT is not very effective in treating severe depression.

12. Recent research suggests that psychodynamic interpersonal therapy may be as effective as the cognitive approach.

13. Genetic studies of families suggest that mood disorders have a genetic basis.

14. Under 10% of successful suicides also involve another psychiatric condition.

15. According to research by Young and others (1994), subjects who were low on Beck's Hopelessness Scale were at highest risk for suicide.

MATCHING

Match the following terms and names with definitions presented below. The answers can be found at the end of the chapter.

a.   postvention
b.   seasonal affective disorder
c.   electroconvulsive shock therapy
d.   cognitive triad
e.   unipolar disorder

f.   schemata
g.   Bowlby
h.   social skills training
i.   lithium
j.   dysthymia

_____ believed depression was a complex reaction to loss
_____ group discussion and intervention following a suicide
_____ includes individuals who have either had one or more episodes of depression but no manic episodes
_____ drug used to treat bipolar disorder I
_____ has been treated using light therapy
_____ focuses on appropriate behavior
_____ involves passing electrical current through patient's head
_____ negative thoughts about self, situation, and future
_____ Beck identified these as thought patterns
_____ "defective or diseased mood"

ANSWER KEY

Multiple Choice

1. b
2. b
3. a
4. c
5. d
6. c
7. b
8. a
9. d
10. b
11. c
12. b

13. a
14. d
15. a
16. d
17. d
18. d
19. d
20. d
21. b
22. d
23. b
24. b

25. c
26. b
27. d
28. b
29. a
30. b
31. a
32. d
33. a
34. c

35. b
36. b
37. a
38. b
39. b
40. a
41. b
42. b
43. a
44. b

True/False

1. T
2. F
3. F
4. T
5. T
6. T
7. T
8. F

9. T
10. T
11. F
12. T
13. T
14. F
15. T

Matching

g
a
e
i
b
h
c
d
f
j

Chapter 11
SCHIZOPHRENIC DISORDER: CHARACTERISTICS AND PROBABLE CAUSES

CHAPTER OVERVIEW

The concept of schizophrenia is highlighted in the present chapter. Definition and characteristic symptoms are presented along with incidence rates, theoretical positions and historical perspectives. The subtypes of disorganized, catatonic, undifferentiated, and paranoid schizophrenia are explained and prognostic factors evaluated. Lastly, therapeutic approaches and their effectiveness are summarized.

CHAPTER OUTLINE

The Impact of Schizophrenic Disorders
Characteristics of Schizophrenic Disorders
      Positive Symptoms
      Negative Symptoms

Major Subtypes of Schizophrenia
What Causes Schizophrenic Disorder?
      Genetic Factors
      Schizophrenic Spectrum Disorders
      Other Biological Factors

Methods of Studying Genetic and Environmental Factors
      Family Studies
      Twin Studies
      Adoption Studies

Vulnerability, Resiliency, and Stress
      Community Factors and Stress
      High-Risk Studies and Search for Markers

LEARNING OBJECTIVES

You should know:

1. the incidence rate of schizophrenia and the diagnostic criteria for it.

2. the characteristics of schizophrenic disorders.

3. the definitions of schizophrenia proposed by Kraepelin and Bleuler. Also be able to describe Schneider's contribution of the idea of first-rank symptoms.

4. the current schizophrenic disorder subtypes and their diagnostic symptoms.

5. the research surrounding proposed causes of schizophrenic disorders.

6. the types of disorders which constitute "schizophrenic spectrum disorders" and their potential relationships to schizophrenia.

7. the various methods used to study genetic and environmental influences on the development of schizophrenic disorders.

8. the diathesis-stress, social-selection, and increased-stress theories of schizophrenia.

KEY TERMS AND CONCEPTS

Following is a list of key terms and concepts that are featured in the chapter and are important for you to know. Write out the definitions of each of these terms and check your answers with the definitions in the text.

schizophrenic disorders
positive symptoms
negative symptoms
delusions
hallucinations
disordered speech
catatonic excitement
catatonic rigidity
paranoid type
catatonic type
disorganized type
undifferentiated type
residual type
monogenic model

expressed
polygenic model
multifactorial polygenic model
schizophrenic spectrum disorders
cerebral ventricles
dopamine hypothesis
assortative mating
discordant
cross-fostering studies
diathesis-stress model
social selection theory
increased-stress theory
communication deviance

CRITICAL THINKING QUESTIONS

In developing answers for the following questions, turn to the section of your chapter that covers the pertinent material. Read each section thoroughly before attempting to frame your answer.

1.   What is a psychosis? List the types of disorders included in this category.

2.   Discuss the epidemiological research findings on schizophrenia and the economic impact of the disorder.

3.   List and briefly describe the major characteristics of a schizophrenic disorder. Differentiate positive from negative symptoms.

4.   What specific subtypes of schizophrenic disorder does DSM-IV recognize? List the unique characteristics of each subtype.

5.   What were Kraepelin and Bleuler's definitions of schizophrenia? How were their perspectives different? What are first and second rank symptoms?

6.   Define the concepts "positive" and "negative" symptoms. How are these used in research?

7.   What are schizophrenic spectrum disorders?

8.   Present the genetic and biological perspectives on schizophrenic disorders.

9.   What methods are used to study genetic and environmental factors in schizophrenia?

10. How do vulnerability, resilience, and stress figure into the complexity of schizophrenia? What information do studies of high-risk factors contribute on the topic?

MULTIPLE CHOICE

The following multiple choice questions will test your comprehension of the material presented in the chapter. Circle the correct choice for each question in the section, then compare your answers with those at the end of the chapter.

1. Schizophrenic disorders are a type of

   a. mood disorder.
   b. insanity.
   c. organic brain syndrome.
   d. psychosis.

2. About _____ percent of the population will be diagnosed as having a schizophrenic disorder in any given year.

   a. 1
   b. 5
   c. 10
   d. 15

3. Individuals diagnosed with a schizophrenic disorder

   a. consume 2 1/2% of total annual health care expenditures in the U.S.
   b. constitute 10% of the permanently and totally disabled population.
   c. make-up 14% of the homeless population in large cities.
   d. all of the above.

4. Which of the characteristics below is not a symptom of schizophrenia?

   a. changes in perception of the environment
   b. difficulty in differentiating oneself from the environment
   c. a change in motivation
   d. pathological lying

5. Often, a family member may notice behavioral changes in a person before the active phase of the schizophrenic episode begins. These symptoms may include impairment in functioning, odd beliefs, lack of interest, and

   a. loss of memory.

b. a decreased concern with personal hygiene.

c. bulimic behavior.

d. waxy flexibility.

6. Select the disorder below that is not a principal psychotic disorder.

a. delusional disorder

b. substance-induced psychotic disorder

c. schizophreniform disorder

d. paranoid personality disorder

7. Which of the following represents a positive symptom for schizophrenia?

a. flattened affect

b. apathy

c. bizarre behavior

d. poverty of speech

8. A delusion is

a. a faulty interpretation of reality.

b. not found in a psychotic disorder.

c. never found in schizophrenia.

d. none of the above.

9. Joe attends a rock concert and is struck by the fact that the singer is referring to him in a number of songs. Joe's belief would be considered a

a. tangential delusion.

b. command delusion.

c. referential delusion.

d. residual delusion.

10. C.T. Harrison, author of an article in *Military Review*, was found

a. to have been misdiagnosed.

b. to be diagnosed as a paranoid schizophrenic.

c. to be competent to stand trial.

d. both a & c

11. Unlike hallucinations experienced in delirium in other disorders, schizophrenics

a. experience them in a clear, conscious state.

b. rarely experience auditory hallucinations.

c. primarily experience tactile hallucinations.

d. hallucinations are not somatic.

12. The theory that intelligence may play a critical role in hallucinations is proposed by

    a. the psychodynamic position.
    b. the cognitive advocates.
    c. the dopamine hypothesis.
    d. rational-emotive proponents.

13. The therapist greets his client by stating, "Good morning, did you sleep well last night?" The client responds, "Yes, but night is when the moon is blue, and sadness brings with it tears of rage, like a lion who stalks the forest to kill." The client's response to this therapist's greeting is most likely due to

    a. hallucinations.
    b. loosening of associations.
    c. delusions.
    d. poverty of content.

14. When we discuss disorganized behavior as it pertains to schizophrenic disorder, we are referring to

    a. problems carrying out activities of daily living.
    b. impaired social functioning.
    c. changes in goal-directed behavior.
    d. all of the above.

15. _____ denotes the lack of movement of a person diagnosed with schizophrenic disorder.

    a. Catatonic rigidity
    b. Catatonic static
    c. Catatonic inexcitement
    d. Catatonic posture

16. Which of the following is not characteristic of a schizophrenic's impaired social functioning?

    a. emotional detachment
    b. violations of personal space
    c. inappropriate sexual behaviors
    d. none of the above

17. According to Baron and others (1992), negative symptoms appear to be associated with

a. a high rate of schizophrenic concordance in other family members.
b. nongenetic causes for schizophrenia.
c. a genetic basis for schizophrenia.
d. an early onset of schizophrenia.

18. Select the term below that is not a DSM-IV subtype of schizophrenic disorder.

a. paranoid
b. undifferentiated
c. hebephrenic
d. disorganized

19. Marty believes that the Communists have planted a radio transmitter in her brain. She claims they are transmitting her thoughts to her neighbors. Marty would most probably be diagnosed as a(n)

a. catatonic schizophrenic.
b. undifferentiated schizophrenic.
c. paranoid schizophrenic.
d. disorganized schizophrenic.

20. Schneider emphasized

a. the importance of developing a reliable classification system.
b. the importance of adequate treatment for the mentally ill.
c. the nature of early childhood experiences in the development of first rank symptoms.
d. the transitional nature of first and second rank symptoms.

21. _____ schizophrenics behave in a childish manner and their behavior appears to be aimless.

a. Paranoid
b. Undifferentiated
c. Simple
d. Disorganized

22. The risk rate for identical twins to develop schizophrenia is

a. exactly 100%.
b. no more than 22%.

c. slightly below 50%.
d. not presently known.

23. The Genain sibling case is illustrative of

a. early childhood sexual abuse and its subsequent consequences.
b. a genetic basis for schizophrenia.
c. the role of NIMH in treating schizophrenia.
d. the relationship between substance abuse and schizophrenia.

24. The study of schizophrenic disorders by genetic theorists has led them to favor a _____ model.

a. monogenic
b. multifactorial polygenic
c. polygenic
d. penetrant

25. The results of using scanning techniques to study the brains of schizophrenics have led to the observation that schizophrenics

a. have significantly larger cerebral ventricles than normals.
b. have more head trauma than normals.
c. brains are smaller in actual size than normals.
d. have less cerebrospinal fluid than normals.

26. The dopamine hypothesis posits that

a. an excess of dopamine at certain synapses is associated with schizophrenia.
b. the schizophrenic's brain lacks dopamine at certain synapses.
c. the development of schizophrenia is related to a deficiency in the number of receptor sites in the brain.
d. none of the above.

27. The studies on D3 as a marker for schizophrenia have

a. been encouraging to geneticists.
b. confounding in their designs which render them uninterpretable.
c. not supported it as a marker for schizophrenia.
d. provided support for its association with schizophrenia.

28. In an NIMH study of identical twins and schizophrenia (Torrey et al., 1994), differences in behavior between twins was noted as early as age

   a. 2.
   b. 5.
   c. 8.
   d. 13.

29. The studies of adoption in Denmark tend to suggest a(n)_____ view of schizophrenic disorders.

   a. environmental
   b. genetic
   c. transpersonal
   d. discordant

30. The diathesis-stress model of schizophrenia hypothesizes

   a. that stress alone is enough to produce a schizophrenic disorder.
   b. that genetics alone will result in schizophrenia.
   c. that schizophrenia is the result of an interaction between genetics and environmental stressors.
   d. none of the above.

31. A recent Swedish study (Lewis et al., 1992) lends support to

   a. the increased-stress theory.
   b. the social-selection theory.
   c. the foster-parent theory.
   d. the immunological theory.

32. The search for early markers for schizophrenia suggests that all of the following are indicators except

   a. impaired attention.
   b. attention dysfunction.
   c. attentional dysfunction associated with adjustment problems in adolescence and adulthood.
   d. over involvement in fantasy.

33. Communication deviance is defined as

    a. the inability to maintain a shared focus of attention during interactions.
    b. the inability to actively express hostile feelings.
    c. the inability to think logically.
    d. the inability to actively participate in an ongoing conversation.

TRUE/FALSE

Indicate whether each statement is true or false. Check your answers at the end of this chapter.

1. In someone experiencing a schizophrenic disorder, a good predictor of outcome is the person's level of adjustment prior to the onset of symptoms.

2. The annual total treatment cost for schizophrenia in the U.S. is $3 million.

3. A schizophrenic may experience foul odors coming from their bodies.

4. According to the psychodynamic perspective, hallucinations represent the freeing of unconscious information.

5. Schizophrenic behavior is often difficult to predict.

6. Paranoid thinking does not tend to fall along a continuum.

7. The cause of schizophrenia is not known.

8. There is evidence to suggest that if a pregnant mother has influenza, the offspring has an increased risk of schizophrenia.

9. Low doses of amphetamines can worsen the symptoms of schizophrenic disorders.

10. Assortative mating refers to marrying someone with dissimilar characteristics.

MATCHING

Match the following terms with information provided below. The answers may be found at the end of the chapter.

a. Kraepelin
b. D1, D2, D3, D4
c. negative symptoms
d. residual type
e. waxy flexibility

f. cross-fostering study
g. social-selection theory
h. disordered speech
i. schizophrenic spectrum disorders
j. assortative mating

_____ loss or decrease in normal functions
_____ loosening of associations
_____ dementia praecox
_____ has negative (or some mild) but not positive symptoms
_____ arm remains in position it is placed
_____ mating with similar partner
_____ includes schizotypal and paranoid personality disorder
_____ dopamine receptor sites in brain
_____ study involving foster children of adoptive, schizophrenic parents
_____ poor coping skills lead to a socioeconomic decline

ANSWER KEY

Multiple Choice

1.d
2.a
3.d
4.d
5.b
6.d
7.c
8.a
9.c
10.b
11.a
12.b
13.b
14.d
15.a
16.d
17.b

18.c
19.c
20.a
21.d
22.c
23.b
24.b
25.a
26.a
27.c
28.b
29.b
30.c
31.a
32.d
33.a

True/False

1. T
2. F
3. T
4. T
5. T

6. F
7. T
8. T
9. T
10. F

Matching

c
h
a
d
e
j
i
b
f
g

Chapter 12
SCHIZOPHRENIC DISORDER: PSYCHOLOGICAL RESEARCH, TREATMENT, AND OUTCOME

CHAPTER OVERVIEW

This chapter surveys the research on attention and information processing as it pertains to the risk of schizophrenic disorder. It also reviews the contribution of therapeutic approaches such as antipsychotic drugs, skills training, family interventions, and community support as interventions. Finally, the results of long-term outcome studies of schizophrenic prognosis are evaluated.

CHAPTER OUTLINE

Attention, Cognition, and the Schizophrenic Process
      Attention Tasks
      Information Processing Tasks
      Thought Disorder

Therapeutic Approaches
      Antipsychotic Drugs
      Skills Training
      Family Interventions
      Community Support

Long-Term Outcome Studies

LEARNING OBJECTIVES

You should know:

1.   what the research on attention and cognition contributes to our understanding of the schizophrenic process.

2.   the various types of tasks used to assess attention and cognition in schizophrenic disorders.

3.   the role of antipsychotic drugs in treating schizophrenic disorders.

4.   the nature and purposes of skills training as they pertain to rehabilitation of the schizophrenic.

5.   the effectiveness of family interventions in preventing relapse and promoting adjustment in schizophrenia.

6.   the role the community plays in helping the schizophrenic to live outside the confines of institutions.

7.   the general findings of long-term outcome studies of schizophrenic disorders.

KEY TERMS AND CONCEPTS

Following is a list of key terms and concepts that are featured in the chapter and are important for you to know. Write out the definitions of each of these terms and check your answers with the definitions in the text.

Continuous Performance Task
smooth-pursuit eye movements
Stroop Task
tardive dyskinesia
social skills training
expressed emotion
milieu therapy
non-residential support

CRITICAL THINKING QUESTIONS

In developing answers for the following questions, turn to the section of your chapter that covers the pertinent material. Read the section thoroughly before attempting to frame your answer.

1.   Discuss the role of attention and information processing in the schizophrenic process. What do the research findings suggest regarding these variables?

2.   What are some of the benefits and limitations of antipsychotic drugs? Are antipsychotic drugs alone effective in treating schizophrenics?

3.   List the types of skills deficits observed in schizophrenics. How effective are the various skills training programs in remediating these deficits.

4. How do family interventions decrease the probability of relapse? Discuss the research on expressed emotion.

5. What components are typically included in a family education program?

6. Review the types of community support provided to schizophrenics. What does the term "milieu therapy" mean?

7. Present the general findings of the long-term outcome studies on schizophrenia.

MULTIPLE CHOICE

The following multiple choice questions will test your comprehension of the material presented in the chapter. Circle the correct choice for each question in the section, then compare your answers with those at the end of the chapter.

1. In a study of attention and reaction time in schizophrenics (Grillon et al., 1990),

   a. schizophrenics demonstrated difficulty ignoring irrelevant stimuli.
   b. schizophrenics were able to screen out irrelevant stimuli.
   c. schizophrenics performed better than normals on a recognition task.
   d. none of the above.

2. Which of the following looks especially promising as a test for a particular biological marker for risk of schizophrenia?

   a. the Continuous Task
   b. eye-tracking measures
   c. Stroop Task
   d. all of the above

3. The Continuous Performance Task may be assessing a dysfunction of

   a. the hypothalamus.
   b. the reticular system of the brain.
   c. the integration of logical thought.
   d. both b & c.

4. Deviant smooth pursuit eye movements

   a. are exclusively seen in schizophrenics.
   b. are not associated with schizophrenic disorders.
   c. are an unreliable measure of cognitive processing.
   d. are also found in people with brain disease.

5.   In a study of disordered cognition and the Rorschach personality test (Solovay et al., 1987),

   a. the control group was rated as having the highest rate of disordered responses.
   b. the manic group displayed the most disordered responses.
   c. the normal group exhibited no disordered responses.
   d. all groups demonstrated some degree of disordered response.

6.   It would appear that _____ may reduce the level of thought disorder in schizophrenics.

   a. cognitive rehabilitation
   b. antipsychotic medication
   c. intensive psychotherapy
   d. social support

7.   The most usual treatment for schizophrenia today is

   a. psychotherapy.
   b. antipsychotic drugs.
   c. ECT.
   d. social skills training.

8.   Despite being on appropriate medication, _____ % of schizophrenics are likely to experience a relapse within one year of discharge from a hospital.

   a. 10
   b. 78
   c. 40
   d. 26

9.   For the most part, _____ is no longer used as a treatment for schizophrenia.

   a. insight-based therapy
   b. psychodynamic therapy
   c. individual therapy
   d. all of the above

10.   Antipsychotic medication does not appear to help the negative symptoms of schizophrenia such as

   a. agitation.
   b. withdrawal.

c. hallucinations.

d. suicidal ideation.

11. About _____ % of discharged schizophrenics stop using their medication.

   a. 80
   b. 25
   c. 50
   d. 3

12. Two reasons cited by Ghaemi and Pope (1994) for the schizophrenics' failure to follow a medication regimen are that patients appear to lack insight into the severity of their illness and

   a. patients may fail to see the relationship between treatment and improved functioning.
   b. may not have the financial resources to obtain medication.
   c. they may view the side-effects as highly aversive.
   d. they may have been discharged prematurely.

13. Tardive dyskinesia is a serious side effect of antipsychotic medication and involves

   a. involuntary movements of the legs.
   b. involuntary movements of mouth and lips.
   c. involuntary recall of traumatic memories.
   d. both a & b.

14. Although clozaril appears to produce improvement in two thirds of patients who were unresponsive to other antipsychotic medication,

   a. it has been associated with bone marrow failure and death in some patients.
   b. the cost of treatment remains high.
   c. the patient's blood levels must be closely monitored.
   d. all of the above.

15. Select the following item which is not a component of social skills training for persons with schizophrenic disorders.

   a. topic selection
   b. eye contact
   c. voice volume
   d. turn-taking

16. Skill areas for symptom management include identifying warning signs of relapse, coping with persistent symptoms, and

    a. negotiating medication issues.
    b. obtaining medication information.
    c. identifying and managing warning signs.
    d. using injectable medication.

17. In a study designed to increase attention span and discrimination ability of schizophrenics (Brenner et al., 1989), after eighteen months of treatment,

    a. the control group performed better than the experimental group.
    b. there was no difference in outcome between the two groups.
    c. schizophrenics showed less symptoms and better attention span than controls.
    d. schizophrenics showed less symptoms and less ability to maintain attention than controls.

18. A mother comments on the behavior of her schizophrenic son by stating, "I suggested he get a part-time job to get his mind off of his troubles. But, he just slammed the door and walked out!" This comment is typical of

    a. flat expressed emotion.
    b. displaced expressed emotion.
    c. negative expressed emotion.
    d. schizogenic emotion.

19. Pick the statement below that is accurate regarding cultural studies of expressed emotion.

    a. Anglo-American families display higher rates of expressed emotion than Indian families.
    b. The Japanese do not show expressed emotion toward schizophrenic relatives.
    c. Traditional Mexican-Americans display lower levels of expressed emotion than do Anglo-Americans.
    d. The rate of expressed emotion for French parents is significantly less than that exhibited by Americans.

20. Family education programs

    a. have been found to prevent relapse/rehospitalization.
    b. have been disappointing in not reducing relapse rates.
    c. do not focus on symptoms of relapse because of a concern about labeling.
    d. are most effective when they occur immediately after a patient's discharge.

21. Choose the stage sequence below that is typical of a schizophrenic relapse.

    a. dysphoric mood, increased stress, psychotic symptoms
    b. dysphoric mood, psychotic symptoms, increased stress.
    c. psychotic symptoms, increased stress, dysphoric mood
    d. increased stress, psychotic symptoms, dysphoric mood

22. Which of the following is not a behavioral intervention used with families who have schizophrenic members?

    a. stress innoculation
    b. goal planning
    c. thought-stopping
    d. education

23. The "first person" story of the twins, Malcom and Michael, clearly illustrates

    a. familial anger toward the system.
    b. that a diagnosis of schizophrenia negatively impacts the family.
    c. how important early intervention is for families.
    d. the positive effect of milieu treatment.

24. Which of the following is not considered to be a goal of milieu therapy?

    a. support and protection
    b. group validation of symptoms
    c. structure and containment
    d. vocational training

25. The concept of nonresidential support could include

    a. providing food stamps to the client.
    b. recruiting a support person.
    c. supplying free medication.
    d. providing the client with feedback on their behavior.

26. All of the following may be early signs of a schizophrenic relapse except

    a. stealing money from family members.
    b. laughing for no apparent reason.
    c. poor personal hygiene.
    d. increased religiosity.

27. Follow-up studies on the outcome of schizophrenia show

a. poor long-term prognosis.
b. that the diagnosis is associated with an increased risk for personal illness.
c. that none of the treatment approaches were consistently beneficial in promoting improvement.
d. all of the above.

28. The Vermont study suggests that schizophrenics may

a. be affected by nutritional changes.
b. be affected by sustained psychosocial changes.
c. be affected by prolonged environmental changes.
d. both b & c.

29. Overall, it appears that what is presently needed most to increase the possibility that a person with schizophrenic disorder will have a positive adjustment after hospitalization is

a. family support
b. continuity of care.
c. skills training.
d. highly skilled crisis teams.

30. Under a comprehensive care program for schizophrenics, rehabilitation refers to

a. housekeeping.
b. nutrition.
c. job training.
d. all of the above.

TRUE/FALSE

Indicate whether each statement is true or false. Check your answers at the end of the chapter.

1. Disruptions of selective attention are a marker for risk of schizophrenia.

2. Deviant smooth eye movement tracking patterns are only found in schizophrenia.

3. A combination of cognitive dysfunction and decrease in coping skills may lead the schizophrenic to experience high levels of social stress.

4. The best treatment for schizophrenia is a combination of antipsychotic drugs and a psychosocial approach.

5. Psychodynamic therapy may provide too much stimulation for persons diagnosed as schizophrenic.

6. Early intervention with drugs appears to improve the long-term outcome for schizophrenia.

7. Ten percent of discharged patients stop taking their medication.

8. Expressed emotion in a family may change over time.

9. There are no clear predictors of what type of psychotic drug will help a given schizophrenic patient.

10. Even psychotic patients have a right to refuse treatment.

11. Social skills training appears to prevent relapse.

12. Research on family interventions was spurred by deinstitutionalization.

13. Foster homes with high expectations also appear to have high positive expressed emotion.

14. Some patients with schizophrenia recover fully.

MATCHING

Match the following terms with information provided below. The answers may be found at the end of the chapter.

a. nonresidential support
b. Stroop Task Performance
c. negative expressed emotion
d. social skills training

e. Kraepelin
f. Milieu therapy
g. eye-tracking
h. Bleuler

_____ noted schizophrenics lacked "acute attention"
_____ provides opportunities for structure and containment
_____ provides missing functions
_____ taps aspect of selective attention
_____ patient asked to follow moving target
_____ based on social learning theory
_____ observed "unsteadiness of attention" in dementia praecox
_____ includes emotional over involvement

ANSWER KEY

Multiple Choice

1. a	16. c
2. d	17. c
3. b	18. c
4. d	19. c
5. d	20. a
6. b	21. b
7. b	22. c
8. c	23. b
9. d	24. d
10. b	25. b
11. c	26. d
12. a	27. d
13. d	28. d
14. d	29. b
15. a	30. a

True/False

1. F	8. T
2. F	9. T
3. T	10. T
4. T	11. F
5. T	12. T
6. T	13. F
7. F	14. T

Matching

h
f
a
b
g
d
e
c

Chapter 13
COGNITIVE IMPAIRMENT DISORDERS

CHAPTER OVERVIEW

Disorders of the brain leading to cognitive, affective, and behavior problems are discussed in this portion of the text. In addition to assessing vulnerability for brain disorders, techniques for determining cognitive dysfunction will be explored. The characteristics of major brain syndromes are reviewed as well as actual/potential causes discussed. Lastly, the contributions of psychological treatment interventions for brain disordered patients are explored.

CHAPTER OUTLINE

The Brain: An Interactional Perspective
       Vulnerability to Brain Disorders
       Assessing Brain Damage
       The Brain and Cognitive Impairment

Delirium
       Delirium Tremens

Dementia
       Alzheimer's Disease
       Pick's Disease
       Huntington's Disease
       Parkinson's Disease
       Brain Trauma: Injuries, Tumors, and Infections

Amnestic Disorders

The Diversity of Cognitive Impairment Disorders
       Cerebral Vascular Disorders
       Korsakoff's Syndrome
       Epilepsy

An Integrative Approach to Brain Disorders

LEARNING OBJECTIVES

You should know:

1. that an interactional perspective on brain disorders is widely accepted. Also, you should be able to discuss the factors that influence vulnerability to brain disorders.

2. the different methods for assessing brain damage, including components of the mental status examination.

3. the symptoms and causes of delirium, and the contribution of alcohol to the onset of delirium tremens.

4. the symptoms and causes of various types of dementia including Alzheimer's disease, Pick's disease, Huntington's disease, and Parkinson's disease.

5. the contributions of injuries, tumors, and infections to brain trauma, as well as the major syndromes associated with each of these factors including AIDS dementia complex and general paresis.

6. that an amnestic disorder is the result of a medical condition or the lingering effects of a chemical substance.

7. the nature and symptoms of cerebral vascular disorders.

8. that certain syndromes such as pellegra or Korsakoff's syndrome are the result of vitamin or nutritional deficiencies.

9. the symptoms of epilepsy and the various types which are common in the U.S.

10. the role of the following treatments in brain disorders: medical, psychodynamic, cognitive, behavioral and community.

KEY TERMS AND CONCEPTS

Following is a list of key terms and concepts that are featured in the chapter and are important for you to know. Write out the definitions of each of these terms and check you answers with the definitions in the text.

mental-status examination
neuropsychologist
syndrome
delirium
delirium tremens

brain deterioration
dementia
senile dementia
presenile dementia
confabulation
primary degeneration dementia
Alzheimer's disease
acetylcholine
Pick's disease
Huntington's disease
Parkinson's disease
traumatic neurosis
syphilitic infections
general paresis
dementia paralytica
amnestic disorders
pellagra
cerebrovascular accidents
strokes
Korsakoff's syndrome
concussions
contusions
lacerations
AIDS dementia complex
Vascular dementia
epilepsy
grand mal seizure
petit mal seizure
psychomotor epilepsy
temporal lobe epilepsy
cerebrovascular strokes
aphasia

CRITICAL THINKING QUESTIONS

In developing answers for the following questions, turn to the section of your chapter that covers the pertinent material. Read the section thoroughly before attempting to frame your answer.

1. What are the factors that influence vulnerability to brain damage and brain disorders? Is an interactional perspective important when considering brain disorders?

2. What are the major procedures used to assess brain damage? What factors are

assessed in a mental status examination?

3. List the deficits associated with delirium. What are the four organic causes of delirium?

4. Describe the symptoms of dementia. Differentiate between senile dementia and pre-senile dementia.

5. What is Alzheimer's disease? Explain its potential physiological causes. Is this disease a major health threat for the U.S.? Describe the impact Alzheimer's disease has on family members and treatment interventions for the patient.

6. Differentiate the following disorders: Pick's disease, Huntington's disease, and Parkinson's disease.

7. AIDS dementia complex is a newly recognized type of dementia. What is it? General paresis is the result of what untreated medical condition?

8. Describe the dimensions of amnestic disorders. Discuss both vascular dementia and Korsakoff's syndrome.

9. Describe the differences among the following disorders: grand mal seizures, petit mal epilepsy, and psychomotor epilepsy. How is epilepsy treated?

10. How have the psychodynamic, behavioral, cognitive and community perspectives contributed to treatment of brain disorders?

MULTIPLE CHOICE

The following multiple choice questions will test your comprehension of the material presented in the chapter. Circle the correct choice for each question in the section, then compare your answers with those at the end of the chapter.

1. Select the factor below that does not influence vulnerability to brain damage and brain disorders.

    a. personal variables
    b. intelligence
    c. social support
    d. age

2.   _____ can often ease adjustment to a brain condition.

    a. A supportive physician
    b. Aphasia
    c. Social support
    d. Social isolation and total bed rest

3.   In order to assess damage or deterioration of the brain, which of the options below may be used?

    a. general physical evaluation
    b. mental status examination
    c. PET scan
    d. all of the above

4.   Which of the following is not generally a part of a mental-status exam?

    a. language
    b. sleep habits
    c. mood
    d. general appearance

5.   Which of the following is able to image the brain in all planes?

    a. a PET scan
    b. a CT scan
    c. an MRI
    d. an x-ray

6.   The most common syndromes involving disorders of the brain and cognitive impairment include disturbances of memory, imagination, thought processing, problem-solving skills, judgement and

    a. identity.
    b. perception.
    c. gait.
    d. fine motor coordination.

7.   A person going through severe withdrawal from alcohol is likely to experience

    a. amnesia.
    b. Pick's disease.
    c. delirium.
    d. primary degeneration dementia.

8.   Which of the following is not one of the general organic causes of delirium?

   a. brain disease
   b. confabulation
   c. intoxication
   d. substance withdrawal

9.   Delirium tremens are characterized by

   a. tremors.
   b. prolonged sleep patterns.
   c. visual hallucinations.
   d. both a. and c.

10.   Which of the following is true about dementia?

   a. Personality changes are rare.
   b. Dementia may be reversible.
   c. Delirium seems to prevent dementia.
   d. Dementia often involves rapid deterioration.

11.   Senile dementia occurs in people

   a. under the age of 70.
   b. under the age of 65.
   c. over the age of 65.
   d. over the age of 70.

12.   In dementia syndromes, confabulation refers to _____ when the person's memory has lapsed.

   a. being unable to recall the names of common objects
   b. filling in memory gaps with inaccurate details
   c. reliving earlier memories
   d. none of the above

13.   Martha is an 82 year old grandmother who was found wandering down the highway by the local police. She did not know where she lived nor the date or time when asked. When the police asked her to come to the local hospital, Martha began screaming hostile insults. Upon arrival at the hospital, Martha was most probably diagnosed as having

   a. Pick's disease.
   b. Alzheimer's disease.

c. Multi-infarct dementia.
d. AIDS dementia.

14. Alzheimer's victims constitute over _____ of all people in nursing homes.

a. 50%
b. 70%
c. 20%
d. 10%

15. The development of plaques and clumps in the brain is associated with

a. Alzheimer's disease.
b. multi-infarct dementia.
c. organic hallucinosis.
d. Huntington's chorea.

16. The only way to be absolutely certain that a person has Alzheimer's disease is to

a. carefully conduct an in-depth mental-status examination.
b. perform a PT scan.
c. perform a PT scan and confirm the diagnosis with a follow-up MRI evaluation.
d. examine the brain after death.

17. _____ disease is associated with a particular form of brain atrophy and its symptoms are very similar to those of Alzheimer's disease.

a. Epilepsy
b. General paresis
c. Huntington's disease
d. None of the above

18. The folk singer and composer Woody Guthrie died at age 55 in 1967 after being misdiagnosed when really suffering from

a. epilepsy.
b. Korsakoff's syndrome.
c. pellagra.
d. Huntington's chorea.

19. By studying the blood of Iris del Valle Soto and other members of her family, researchers

a. have identified the location on chromosome pair 4 where the Huntington gene is located.

b. have developed a diagnostic genetic test to screen for Huntington's disease.
c. have shown that Huntington's disease is not genetically transmitted.
d. both a & b.

20.   In patients with _____, the most prominent symptoms are dementia, irritability, depression, hallucinations, delusions and choreiform movements.

a. Huntington's disease
b. Pick's disease
c. AIDS dementia
d. Alzheimer's disease

21.   Research on Parkinson's disease

a. suggests that brain cell implantation may be an effective treatment.
b. raises ethical issues by considering "sham surgery".
c. focuses on increased production of dopamine.
d. all of the above.

22.   Traumatic neurosis refers to

a. reactions that come after a startling event.
b. a neurotic who has a psychogenic head injury.
c. the damaging of neurons due to head injury.
d. PTSD when it occurs because of head injury.

23.   Major tears or ruptures in the brain tissue are called

a. lacerations.
b. concussions.
c. contusions.
d. intracranial adhesions.

24.   Which of the following is true regarding AIDS dementia complex?

a. It closely resembles psychological depression.
b. ADC is reversible.
c. It is seen only in the last stages of life.
d. A positive test for HIV means that individuals also have ADC.

25.   One of the results of untreated syphilis in its late stage is

a. seizures.
b. general paresis.
c. pellagra.

d. choreiform movements.

26. Amnestic disorders may be defined as disturbances of memory due to the effects of a medical condition or

   a. chronic tumor.
   b. the persistent effects of a chemical substance.
   c. cerebrovascular stroke.
   d. none of the above.

27. Multi-infarct dementia is another name for

   a. epilepsy.
   b. pellegra.
   c. hypertensive dementia.
   d. vascular dementia.

28. Korsakoff's syndrome is characterized by the loss of recent and past memories and an inability to form new memories. Which of the following is most likely to be diagnosed as having this disorder?

   a. a schizophrenic
   b. an anorectic
   c. a chronic alcoholic
   d. an epileptic

29. Which of the following is caused by a dietary deficiency?

   a. Parkinson's disease
   b. general paresis
   c. dementia paralytica
   d. pellagra

30. The most severe form of epilepsy is

   a. grand mal.
   b. petit mal.
   c. psychomotor.
   d. posttraumatic.

31. Which of the following is not one of the major ways to treat epilepsy?

   a. phenobarbitol
   b. antipsychotic medication

c. psychological management

d. surgery

32. The majority of epileptics

a. have the same intellectual abilities as the general population.

b. suffer mild disturbances in psychological functioning in between seizures.

c. seldom have a warning that a seizure is about to occur.

d. often suffer from hallucinations and periods of unpredictable behavior.

33. When treating the organic brain disorders, behavioral psychologists

a. focus on such factors as personality and early experiences as an indicator of how much a person might recover.

b. focus on people's ability to adapt and learn new responses.

c. teach the patient memory-aiding techniques and help relieve depression associated with dementia.

d. leave the treatment methods to the neurologists in this case.

TRUE/FALSE QUESTIONS

Indicate whether each statement is true or false. Check your answers at the end of this chapter.

1. A person's adaptation to brain disorders is highly idiosyncratic.

2. Behavioral deficits caused by brain injury in childhood may not be noticed until later on in life.

3. Stress, sensory and sleep deprivation, and severe fatigue contribute to the onset of delirium.

4. Delirium tremens is not life-threatening.

5. Depressive features are not typically seen in dementia.

6. The leading cause of mental deterioration among the elderly is Alzheimer's disease.

7. Alzheimer's and Pick's disease appears to have a genetic basis.

8. Traumatic brain injury is a common cause of mental disorder.

9. A person may expect to recover from a concussion in about 4 or 5 weeks.

10. Because AIDS dementia occurs in younger people, the disorder may be misdiagnosed.

11. An epileptic seizure appears to be the result of an "electrical storm" in the brain.

12. Petit mal seizures are obvious and therefore easy to identify.

13. Cases of brain damage are highly concentrated in the segment of the population with low socioeconomic status.

MATCHING

Match the following terms with information provided below. The answers may be found at the end of the chapter.

a. grand mal seizure   f. confabulation
b. Pick's disease   g. delirium
c. contusions   h. mental-status examination
d. amnestic syndrome   i. syphilitic infection
e. pellagra   j. Neuropsychologist

_____ rupturing of tiny blood vessels
_____ has symptoms very similar to Alzheimer's disease
_____ loss of consciousness and extreme spasms
_____ may lead to irreversible brain disorders
_____ detailed but inaccurate memories
_____ caused by a deficiency of the vitamin niacin
_____ an interview
_____ specialist in assessment of cognitive dysfunction in brain disorders
_____ symptoms include disorientation, confusion and cognitive impairment
_____ memory difficulty involving inability to learn new material or recall information acquired in the past

ANSWER KEY

Multiple Choice

1.b	18.d
2.c	19.d
3.d	20.a
4.b	21.d
5.b	22.a
6.b	23.a
7.c	24.a
8.b	25.b
9.d	26.b
10.b	27.d
11.c	28.c
12.b	29.d
13.b	30.a
14.a	31.b
15.a	32.a
16.d	33.b
17.d	

True/False

1. T	8. T
2. T	9. F
3. T	10. T
4. F	11. T
5. F	12. F
6. T	13. T
7. T	

Matching

c
b
a
i
f
e
h
j
g
d

Chapter 14
SUBSTANCE-RELATED DISORDERS

CHAPTER OVERVIEW

This chapter introduces you to the topic of substance-related disorders. Alcohol abuse and dependence issues are reviewed; treatment strategies and prevention programs delineated. Other drugs including barbiturates, opioids, cocaine, amphetamines, hallucinogens, cannabis, nicotine and caffeine are also discussed in terms of addictive properties, physiological impact and therapeutic interventions.

CHAPTER OUTLINE

Substance-Use Disorders
       Substance Dependence
       Substance Abuse

Substance-Induced Disorders
Alcohol-Related Disorders
       Excessive Alcohol Use
       Perspectives on Alcohol-Related Disorders
       Treatment
       Preventing Alcohol-Related Disorders

Other Drugs
       Barbiturates and Tranquilizers
       The Opiods
       Cocaine
       Amphetamines
       Inhalants
       Hallucinogens
       Phencyclidine (PCP)
       Cannabis
       Nicotine
       Caffeine

Substance Dependence and Social Policy

LEARNING OBJECTIVES

You should know:

1. the scope of substance-abuse problems in the U.S.

2. the difference between "substance abuse" and substance dependence", and their respective criteria. You should also be able to provide definitions for tolerance, withdrawal and compulsive substance use.

3. the unique characteristics of alcohol abuse and dependence, and be able to provide facts about gender differences and the problem of alcohol in the U.S.

4. the impact alcohol has on human physiology, and the risks it presents.

5. what theoretical perspectives exist regarding alcohol addiction, including the controversy between the value of total abstinence versus controlled drinking.

6. the various treatment interventions used for alcohol abuse.

7. the mechanisms of action and symptoms of barbiturate and tranquilizer usage.

8. the effects of opiod drugs and the theoretical perspectives of exposure orientation versus interactional orientation.

9. the effects of cocaine and amphetamines on physiology, and treatment measures for abuse/dependence. Also know what effects cocaine abuse has on newborns.

10. what effects PCP, LSD and marijuana has on the body, and what is meant by a "post-hallucinogen perceptual disorder".

11. the major effects that both nicotine and caffeine have on physiological functioning.

KEY TERMS AND CONCEPTS

Following is a list of key terms and concepts that are featured in the chapter and are important for you to know. Write out the definitions of each of these terms and check your answers with the definitions in the text.

psychoactive drugs
substance dependence
tolerance
withdrawal
compulsive substance use

substance intoxication
substance-induced disorders
alcohol
physiological dependence
alcohol intoxication
problem drinking
fetal alcohol syndrome
oral-dependent personality
detoxification
aversive conditioning
controlled drinking
relapse-prevention programs
abstinence-violation effect
barbiturates
opiod
endorphins
enkephalins
dynorphins
opiate
morphine
heroin
narcotics
exposure orientation
interactional orientation
methadone maintenance
naltrexone
cocaine
crack
supportive psychotherapy
amphetamines
hallucinogens
lysergic acid diethylamide (LSD)
post-hallucinogen perceptual disorder
phencyclidine (PCP)
marijuana
hashish
nicotine

CRITICAL THINKING QUESTIONS

In developing answers for the following questions, turn to the section of your chapter that covers the pertinent material. Read the section thoroughly before attempting to frame your answer.

1. Differentiate substance dependence disorders from substance abuse disorders. Define intoxication, withdrawal, and flashbacks.

2. Define addictive behavior and tolerance.

3. What is alcohol abuse? List some facts about the problems of alcohol. Explain the concepts problem drinking and alcoholism.

4. What effects does alcohol have on the body and mental health?

5. Present the biological, psychodynamic, and learning perspectives on alcoholism.

6. What cognitive factors have been related to problem drinking?

7. How may social conditions and community factors contribute to excessive use of alcohol? Present the "addictive cycle" of the interactional model.

8. What is detoxification? List the symptoms of withdrawal.

9. Contrast the biological and community approaches to the treatment of alcoholism.

10. Discuss the learning and cognitive models of alcoholism.

11. Discuss alcohol abuse and relapse prevention.

12. Briefly describe opioids as a psychoactive drug and discuss their addictive potential. What treatment strategies are available for this addiction?

13. Delineate the effects and treatment of cocaine addiction.

14. Describe the characteristics associated with the use of amphetamines, LSD, PCP, and marijuana.

15. What are the withdrawal symptoms of nicotine? Describe the treatments available for smoking addiction.

16. How addictive is caffeine?

MULTIPLE CHOICE

The following multiple choice questions will test your comprehension of the material presented in the chapter. Circle the correct choice for each question in the section, then compare your answers with those at the end of the chapter.

1. Psychoactive substances

   a. are used by only a small minority of the population.
   b. have very different effects than the medications typically prescribed by a physician.
   c. cause psychotic-like symptoms.
   d. affect thoughts, emotions, and behaviors.

2. A government survey in 1993 showed that _____ million Americans were drug abusers.

   a. 2
   b. 11.7
   c. 7.7
   d. 2.9

3. Physiological dependence on a substance can be shown in two ways:

   a. tolerance or withdrawal.
   b. tolerance or repeated intoxication.
   c. frequent and continued use of the substance.
   d. a "high" feeling and withdrawal symptoms.

4. Compulsive substance abuse involves

   a. drug-seeking behavior.
   b. ingestion or use of substances.
   c. hiding alcohol and other drugs.
   d. both a & b.

5. DSM-IV

   a. does not consider physiological dependence in its consideration of disorders.
   b. distinguishes between substance abuse and dependence.
   c. reports that there is no difference between substance abuse and substance dependence.
   d. none of the above.

6. Which of the following is not an indication of substance intoxication?

   a. mania
   b. perceptual problems
   c. wakefulness
   d. judgement problems

7. Which of the following is the only type of alcohol safe for human consumption?

   a. isopropyl
   b. ethyl alcohol
   c. wood alcohol
   d. methyl alcohol

8. Betty has been drinking until she has reached a blood/alcohol level of .50. You would expect her to

   a. show uninhibited and silly behaviors.
   b. have problems with reasoning powers, memory and judgment.
   c. have poor motor coordination, and stagger when walking.
   d. possibly die.

9. A 220-pound man has four alcoholic drinks at happy hour. Is he intoxicated?

   a. no
   b. maybe
   c. probably
   d. yes

10. Children with fetal alcohol syndrome

    a. usually become alcoholics like their parents.
    b. are often mentally retarded.
    c. have a high incidence of childhood leukemia.
    d. are often born with alcohol in their bloodstreams.

11. The greatest and most immediate effects of alcohol are on the

    a. central nervous system.
    b. liver.
    c. stomach.
    d. sense organs.

12.   There is evidence of a high prevalence of sensitivity to alcohol among
        people of _____ derivation.

        a. Eastern European
        b. Latin American
        c. Asian
        d. Swedish

13.   According to the psychodynamic view, which would NOT be a characteristic of the
        oral-dependent personality?

        a. self-doubt
        b. passivity
        c. depression
        d. dependence

14.   Most researchers agree that alcohol is

        a. an unconditioned response.
        b. a punishing stimulus.
        c. a reinforcer.
        d. a negative reinforcer.

15.   Which of the following is not one of the cultural conditions that minimize alcohol
        problems?

        a. Alcohol is not used at all in the family.
        b. Children are exposed to alcohol at an early age in family settings.
        c. Alcohol is considered a food and usually served with meals.
        d. Abstinence is socially acceptable but intoxication is not.

16.   When a person is intoxicated
        a. black coffee can be an effective way to "sober him/her up."
        b. a very cold shower can be an effective sobering agent.
        c. making the person walk around in fresh air can be an effective sobering
        agent.
        d. there is no effective sobering agent.

17.   During therapy Jim, who is a problem drinker, is told to visualize that he is about to
        drink some alcohol. Then he imagines he is feeling nauseous and feels like vomiting.
        This type of technique is called

        a. aversive conditioning.
        b. covert sensitization.
        c. systematic desensitization.

d. disulfiram therapy.

18. Relapse-prevention programs and concern about the abstinence-violation effect is most likely to be part of

    a. the psychodynamic approach to treatment of alcohol problems.
    b. the Alcoholics Anonymous approach to treatment of alcoholism.
    c. the cognitive approach to treating problem drinking behavior.
    d. detoxification.

19. Which of the following is not a way your text suggests that students can help themselves before they drink?

    a. select a designated driver
    b. pace drinks to 3 per hour
    c. focus an event on something other than drinking
    d. have non-alcoholic drinks available

20. A natural opioid produced by the brain is (are)

    a. hallucinogens.
    b. barbiturates.
    c. endorphins.
    d. methadone.

21. Heroin is a derivative of

    a. morphine.
    b. marijuana.
    c. endorphins.
    d. none of the above.

22. The opiates cause mood changes, sleepiness, metal dulling, and

    a. hyperventilation.
    b. appetite loss.
    c. depression of the brain's respiratory center.
    d. both a & c.

23. The ability of American service personnel in Vietnam to so easily leave heavy drug use behind when they returned to the U.S. is best explained by

    a. the exposure orientation.
    b. the interactional-orientation.
    c. the methadone maintenance approach to drug addiction.

d. successful detoxification techniques.

24. Which of the following is not one of the effects of cocaine?

   a. euphoria
   b. feelings of separation from one's body
   c. increased heart rate
   d. increased energy

25. Estimates of the number of "crack babies" born each year ranges from _____ to _____.

   a. 20,000; 50,000
   b. 50,000; 120,000
   c. 200,000; 500,000
   d. 50,000; 200,000

26. The effects of _____ are produced with as little as 50 micrograms of the substance.

   a. cocaine
   b. amphetamines
   c. LSD
   d. PCP

27. A predominant feature of post-hallucinogen perceptual disorder is

   a. loss of time.
   b. loss of depth perception.
   c. rapid eye movements.
   d. flashbacks.

28. _____ is (are) classified as a dissociative anesthetic.

   a. Cocaine
   b. Amphetamines
   c. LSD
   d. PCP

29. Which of the following is not true of marijuana?

   a. It suppresses male hormones.
   b. It can cause harm to an unborn child.
   c. It can damage chromosomes.
   d. It can be secreted in breast milk.

30.   Select the term below that is not a stage of change in smoking cessation.

     a. action
     b. maintenance
     c. contemplation and commitment
     d. continuance

TRUE/FALSE QUESTIONS

Indicate whether each statement is true or false. Check your answers at the end of this chapter.

1.   Teens' use of alcohol and marijuana appear to be on the increase.

2.   The term "addiction" is not used in the DSM-IV.

3.   People differ in their vulnerabilities to the negative side effects of particular substances.

4.   Seventy percent of all traffic fatalities are alcohol related.

5.   Moderate use of alcohol may lessen the chance of heart attack.

6.   There does not appear to be a genetic basis for alcoholism.

7.   The effects of barbiturates and alcohol are addictive.

8.   Endorphins are natural opiates.

9.   Methadone maintenance's popularity as a form of treatment has decreased in recent years.

10.   Naltrexone blocks opiod receptors.

11.   The use of inhalants to "get high" includes the use of gasoline and lighter fluid.

12.   Caffeine is the world's most widely used mind-altering drug.

MATCHING

Match the following terms with information provided below. The answers may be found at the end of the chapter.

a. morphine
b. exposure orientation
c. barbiturates
d. interactional orientation
e. abstinence-violation effect

f. cocaine
g. naltrexone
h. PCP
i. Inhalants
j. detoxification

_____ drug used by Freud
_____ important factor in relapse
_____ prescribed for anxiety relief or to prevent convulsions
_____ drug used to treat opioid addiction
_____ a dissociative anesthetic
_____ most important active ingredient of opium
_____ considers both the person and situation in development of addiction
_____ "drying out"
_____ addiction is a function of mere exposure to opioids
_____ examples include gasoline and aerosol sprays

ANSWER KEY

Multiple Choice

1.d

2.b

3.a

4.d

5.b

6.a

7.b

8.d

9.b

10.b

11.a

12.c

13.c

14.c

15.a

16.d

17.a

18.c

19.b

20.c

21.a

22.c

23.b

24.b

25.d

26.c

27.d

28.d

29.c

30.d

True/False

1.T	7.T
2.T	8.T
3.T	9.F
4.F	10.T
5.T	11. T
6.F	12. T

Matching

f
e
c
g
h
a
d
j
b
i

Chapter 15
DISORDERS OF CHILDHOOD AND ADOLESCENCE

CHAPTER OVERVIEW

Disorders of childhood and adolescence are presented in this chapter. Among those discussed are: behavior disorders, conduct disorders and emotional disturbances. Attention-deficit/hyperactivity disorder is highlighted with emphasis given to effective treatment strategies. Eating disorders and depression are also surveyed and therapeutic interventions used with children and adolescents evaluated.

CHAPTER OUTLINE

The Scope of the Problem
        Persistence of Childhood Disorders

Disruptive Behavior
        Attention-Deficit/Hyperactivity Disorder
        Oppositional Defiant Disorder and Conduct Disorder

Internalizing Disorders
        Separation Anxiety Disorder
        Overanxious Disorder of Childhood
        Fears and Phobias
        Obsessive-Compulsive Disorder
        Depression

Eating Disorders
        Anorexia Nervosa
        Bulimia Nervosa

Therapy for Children and Adolescents
        Play Therapy
        Behavioral and Cognitve-Behavioral Therapy
        Family Therapy
        Results of Therapy

LEARNING OBJECTIVES

You should know:

1.   the scope of childhood/adolescent disorders in the U.S. and that problems of childhood often persist into adulthood.

2.   the characteristics, treatment interventions and possible etiological factors of attention-deficit/hyperactivity disorder.

3.   the nature, characteristics and long-term effects of physical child abuse and child sexual abuse.

4.   the diagnostic criteria for oppositional defiant disorder and conduct disorder.

5.   the various types of "internalizing disorders" discussed in your text and their etiologies and treatment paradigms.

6.   the different types of eating disorders observed in children. Also, you should be able to explain the nature, prevalence, etiology and treatment models used in anorexia and bulimia.

7.   that a variety of treatment protocols are used with adolescents and children, and which ones seem to be especially successful in treating specific disorders.

8.   the factors implicated in successful assessment, diagnosis and treatment of children and adolescents from diverse cultural backgrounds.

KEY TERMS AND CONCEPTS

Following is a list of key terms and concepts that are featured in the chapter and are important for you to know. Write out the definitions of each of these terms and check your answers with the definitions in the text.

child abuse
sexual abuse
attention-deficit/hyperactivity disorder (A-D/HD)
conduct disorder
oppositional defiant disorder
internalizing disorders
separation anxiety disorder
over anxious disorder of childhood
symbolic modeling
obsessive-compulsive behaviors

ritualistic behavior
pica
rumination disorder of infancy
anorexia nervosa
bulimia nervosa
binge-purge cycle
play therapy
meta-analysis

CRITICAL THINKING QUESTIONS

In developing answers for the following questions, turn to the section of your chapter that covers the pertinent material. Read the section thoroughly before attempting to frame your answer.

1.   How do behavioral problems impact a child's development?

2.   Differentiate between child sexual abuse and child abuse. List some potential results of child abuse. What prevalence rates are cited in the test?

3.   What are the characteristics associated with attention-deficit/hyperactivity disorder?

4.   Describe the possible causes of attention-deficit/hyperactivity disorder. What treatments are used?

5.   Explain the term "conduct disorder" listing clinical features. Contrast this with the term "oppositional defiant disorder". Review characteristics and treatment strategies for these disorders.

6.   Explain the nature of internalizing disorders. List the most common internalizing disorders seen in children and their symptoms.

7.   What are the characteristic signs of depression in girls and boys? Discuss the causes of depressive disorders in children and adolescents.

8.   Is suicide a real concern for parents of young children and adolescents? What therapeutic approaches are used to treat depressed children and adolescents?

9.   Define anorexia nervosa. List characteristics of the disorder. What are the causes and consequences of the disorder, and how is it treated?

10.   Bulimia nervosa has a "binge-purge" cycle as a disorder characteristic. Explain this. How is bulimia treated?

11. Why is it most effective in many cases to treat the parent rather than the child? What purposes does this focus serve?

12. Describe the therapies used to treat children and adolescents.

13. What factors are especially crucial for the treatment of children and adolescents from diverse cultural backgrounds?

MULTIPLE CHOICE

The following multiple choice questions will test your comprehension of the material presented in the chapter. Circle the correct choice for each question in the section, then compare your answers with those at the end of the chapter.

1. Pathological development may be thought of as

   a. a simple retardation of cognitive development.
   b. a deficiency in growth and integration of competencies.
   c. a failure to maintain separate competencies.
   d. both b & c.

2. Select the statement below which is incorrect.

   a. Behavioral problems may interfere with development by delaying academic and social learning.
   b. Withdrawn children are less likely to be referred to a mental health specialist than an active child.
   c. Parents may feel guilty about a child who exhibits maladaptive behavior.
   d. Reading problems are not associated with underlying pathology.

3. Select the best estimate of children under 18 years of age who meet the criteria for one or more mental disorder.

   a. 10-12%
   b. 6-8%
   c. 17-22%
   d. 2-3%

4. What percentage of children who need help for maladaptive behavior receive it?

   a. 23%
   b. 18%
   c. 14%
   d. 16%

5. Which of the following is not a risk factor for childhood disorders?

    a. low socioeconomic status
    b. parental psychopathology
    c. family discord
    d. low birth weight

6. One reason researchers believe that childhood disorders are distinct from disorders of adulthood is that

    a. childhood disorders tend to have brief durations.
    b. sex ratios for these disorders switch from childhood to adulthood.
    c. the symptoms tend to be dramatically different.
    d. disorders of childhood appear to incorporate developmental milestones as themes.

7. Warren is easily distracted, fails to pay close attention to the teacher's instructions and often leaves his assigned desk in the second grade classroom. Warren's behavior is indicative of

    a. pica.
    b. attention-deficit/hyperactivity disorder.
    c. oppositional deficit disorder.
    d. an internalizing disorder.

8. Which of the following is not one of the categories where A-D/HD children show inappropriate behaviors for their ages?

    a. destructiveness
    b. impulsiveness
    c. inattention
    d. hyperactivity

9. The three types of A-D/HD include the inattentive type, the hyperactive-impulsive type, and the

    a. contained type.
    b. constitutional type.
    c. convoluted type.
    d. combined type.

10. The I.Q.'s of abused children

   a. are lower than expected.
   b. are bigger than expected.
   c. are unaffected by the abuse.
   d. are much higher than those of neglected children.

11. Which of the responses below is not typically seen in sexually abused children?

   a. stigmatization
   b. traumatization
   c. betrayal
   d. detachment

12. _____ percent of sexually abused children do not evidence psychopathology when assessed by standard measures.

   a. 30-50
   b. 10-50
   c. 20-50
   d. 40-50

13. Prevalence estimates for A-D/HD range from _____ percent of school age children and constitute _____ percent of referrals to child clinics.

   a. 3-5; 30-40
   b. 7-12; 10-30
   c. 4-5; 30-40
   d. 2-10; 20-30

14. The study cited in the text that involved A-D/HD children as "negative social catalysts" found that these children

   a. lacked appropriate socialization.
   b. elicited maladaptive behaviors from others around them.
   c. use their social skills in a negative fashion.
   d. regress in social situations.

15. The research study involving simulation of an astronaut and mission control revealed that A-D/HD boys

   a. lacked enough attention to play the game.
   b. had difficulty learning by observation of models.
   c. were more enthusiastic about the game than controls.
   d. none of the above.

16.   Select the statement which best summarizes the research on the causes of attention-deficit/hyperactivity disorder.

a. A genetic cause has been found.
b. The cause appears to be environmental.
c. Birth defects cause the disorder.
d. The causes are unknown.

17.   The most common treatment for hyperactive children is

a. tranquilizers.
b. stimulant medication.
c. mainstreaming.
d. amniocentesis.

18.   Research on therapeutic intervention for attention-deficit/hyperactivity disorder has demonstrated that

a. behavioral therapies work best.
b. drugs alone are effective.
c. psychodynamic therapies are the most effective.
d. drugs and behavioral interventions are most effective.

19.   William's mother describes his behavior in the following manner: resentful, defiant, argumentative in interactions, and irritable. These symptoms suggest the presence of a(n)

a. anxiety disorder of childhood.
b. oppositional defiant disorder.
c. disruptive disorder.
d. obsessive-compulsive disorder.

20.   Children who develop conduct disorders before age 10 are more likely to develop _____ in adulthood.

a. aggressive personality disorder
b. antisocial personality disorder
c. paranoid personality disorder
d. schizotypal personality disorder

21. Select a typical prevention measure for conduct disorder from the list of strategies below.

   a. a project designed to improve an adolescent's social skill
   b. group therapy for parents of children diagnosed as having conduct disorders
   c. a project designed to enhance preschoolers' creativity
   d. none of the above

22. Which of the following is not considered to be an internalizing disorder?

   a. separation anxiety
   b. phobias
   c. A-D/HD
   d. depression

23. Obsessions involve _____, while compulsions are described as

   a. rituals; thoughts.
   b. thoughts; rituals.
   c. dreams; thoughts.
   d. thoughts; fears.

24. Of the following, which is true of separation anxiety disorder?

   a. Treatment failure is often due to parents' inability to comply with the treatment program.
   b. It has a physiological basis.
   c. It is best treated with drugs.
   d. Children with this disorder usually become agoraphobic.

25. Overanxious disorder of childhood is analagous to _____ in adults.

   a. separation anxiety disorder
   b. dependent personality disorder
   c. dysthymia
   d. none of the above

26. Which of the following is not a common symptom of depression in girls?

   a. eating erratically
   b. feeling ugly
   c. being unhappy about social life
   d. denying being unhappy

27. A questionnaire that is often used to screen children for depression is the

   a. Daily Depression Scale.
   b. Affective Checklist for Kids.
   c. Emotional Factor Inventory.
   d. Children's Depression Inventory.

28. _____ is an eating disorder in which a child consistently eats inedible substances.

   a. Anorexia nervosa
   b. Pica
   c. Failure to thrive syndrome
   d. Bulimia nervosa

29. Anorexia may lead to

   a. dry skin.
   b. death.
   c. cardiac arrhythmia.
   d. all of the above.

30. One theory of anorexia posits that it may result in biologically vulnerable persons who have a defensive self-concept and

   a. focus on thinness as a means of self-worth and success.
   b. experience high levels of depression.
   c. lack normal levels of serotonin.
   d. both a & b.

31. Bulimia is not simply an eating problem, it also involves

   a. suicidal thoughts.
   b. cognitive distortions.
   c. poor overall adjustment.
   d. schizophrenic hallucinations.

32. The most frequently used method to treat children with maladaptive behaviors is

   a. behavioral therapy.
   b. family therapy.
   c. play therapy.
   d. peer therapy.

33. A meta-analysis conducted on the effects of therapy on children and adolescents (Weisz et al., 1992) found overall

   a. that clients who received treatment functioned better than controls.
   b. that therapy had no long-term effects.
   c. that the type of therapy used was the most important predictor of outcome.
   d. that therapy had no discernible effect at follow-up.

TRUE/FALSE QUESTIONS

Indicate whether each statement is true or false. Check your answers at the end of this chapter.

1. Abused children have a very high rate of psychological problems.

2. In order to diagnose A-D/HD, symptoms must be observed after age seven.

3. Physically abused children have poor peer relations.

4. Most children are sexually abused by people they know.

5. Success at socially interacting with peers is one of the most important aspects of child development.

6. Research has indicated a potential problem in the area of the corpus collosum in children with A-D/HD.

7. Medicated A-D/HD children have better prognoses in the future than non-medicated A-D/HD children.

8. A-D/HD criteria have been modified so that they also apply to adults.

9. Conduct disorders are found predominately in females.

10. If separation anxiety disorder begins in adolescence, it may result in substantial psychopathology.

11. Symbolic modeling is not effective as a treatment for fears and phobias.

12. For kids with obsessive-compulsive disorders, Prozac has been used with some success.

13. The peak risk period for depression is mid- and late adolescence.

14. Approximately 52% of persons with anorexia are female.

15. Antidepressant medications are not very effective in treating anorexia.

16. The most effective approach to therapy for young children is to work with the parent instead of the child.

MATCHING

Match the following terms with information provided below. The answers may be found at the end of the chapter.

a. pica
b. symbolic modeling
c. conduct disorder
d. hyperactivity
e. separation anxiety disorder

f. child abuse
g. play therapy
h. bulimia nervosa
i. ritualistic behaviors
j. internalizing disorder

_____ may involve harming animals
_____ may be a normal part of child development
_____ involves purging
_____ child shows excessive anxiety when not with parent
_____ includes jumping around and wiggling when sitting down
_____ used to help children act-out their feelings
_____ conditions characterized by anxiety and depression
_____ realistic situations used to reduce anxiety
_____ includes the use of severe punishment
_____ eating non-food substances

ANSWER KEY

Multiple Choice

1.b	9.d
2.d	10.a
3.c	11.d
4.b	12.c
5.d	13.a
6.b	14.b
7.b	15.b
8.a	16.d

17.b

18.d

19.b

20.b

21.a

22.c

23.b

24.a

25.d

26.d

27.d

28.b

29.d

30.a

31.b

32.a

33.a

True/False

1. T

2. F

3. T

4. T

5. T

6. T

7. F

8. T

9. F

10. T

11. F

12. T

13. T

14. F

15. T

16. T

Matching

c

i

h

e

d

g

j

b

f

a

Chapter 16
DEVELOPMENTAL DISORDERS

CHAPTER OVERVIEW

This chapter reviews two forms of developmental disorders: autism and mental retardation. The characteristics, etiology and courses of the disorders are presented and research findings and current issues discussed. The effect of legislation is highlighted as it applies to mental retardation, and the impact of retardation upon the family is reviewed.

CHAPTER OUTLINE

Autistic Disorder
>Characteristics of Autistic Behavior
>Research on Autistic Disorder
>Therapy
>Prospects for Change

Mental Retardation
>Degrees of Mental Retardation
>Biological Causes of Mental Retardation
>Psychosocial Disadvantage
>Psychosocial Enrichment
>Psychological and Social Problems
>The Families of Retarded Children

LEARNING OBJECTIVES

You should know:

1.	the characteristics of autism.

2.	the differences between autism and childhood schizophrenia.

3.	the nature of cognitive, social, and affective deficits found in autism.

4.	what biological factors have been implicated in the origin of autism.

5.	the role of behavior modification as a therapeutic intervention in autism.

6.   the four levels of mental retardation and the skill areas in which retarded persons experience deficits.

7.   the differences between autism and mental retardation.

8.   biological factors implicated in the origin of autism.

9.   the nature and causes of Down syndrome.

10.   what is meant by psychosocial disadvantage as it pertains to retardation and the effects of psychosocial enrichment on the functioning of individuals.

11.   the psychological and social problems experienced by retarded persons.

12.   the impact of mental retardation on the family.

KEY TERMS AND CONCEPTS

Following is a list of key terms and concepts that are featured in the chapter and are important for you to know. Write out the definitions of each of these terms and check your answers with the definitions in the text.

autistic disorder
echolalia
mental retardation
psychosocially disadvantaged
hereditary
mutants
innate
congenital
constitutional
tuberous sclerosis
phenylketonuria
Tay-Sachs disease
Fragile X syndrome
autosomes
chromosomal abnormality
Down syndrome
trisomy 21
trisomy 13
trisomy 18
amniocentesis
rubella virus
fetal alcohol syndrome

asphyxia
prematurity
mainstreamed

CRITICAL THINKING QUESTIONS

In developing answers for the following questions, turn to the section of your chapter that covers the pertinent material. Read the section the section thoroughly before attempting to frame your answer.

1. What are the characteristics of autism?

2. Describe the research on autism. What types of therapeutic approaches are used to treat autism?

3. What is mental retardation and how is it distinguished from autism?

4. Describe the characteristics of mild, moderate, severe, and profound mental retardation.

5. What are the different genetic causes of mental retardation?

6. Describe the features and causes of Down syndrome.

7. What prenatal environmental factors can result in mental retardation?

8. What are the characteristics and causes of fetal alcohol syndrome?

9. What problems at and after birth can increase the probability of mental retardation?

10. Explain the concept of "psychosocial disadvantage" and "psychosocial enrichment". Discuss the research findings of the latter.

11. What types of social and psychological problems do the retarded experience in daily living?

12. Define the concept of mainstreaming. Discuss research findings on this topic.

13. Discuss the impact of mental retardation on the family.

MULTIPLE CHOICE

The following multiple choice questions will test your comprehension of the material presented in the chapter. Circle the correct choice for each question in the section, then compare your answers with those at the end of the chapter.

1. Which of the following is not a clinical feature of autism?

   a. lack of awareness of others
   b. speech abnormalities
   c. insistence on sameness
   d. psychotic features

2. Leo Kanner (1943) first described autism as "extreme autistic aloneness" and

   a. an aversion to language.
   b. clinging dependency.
   c. an obsession for sameness.
   d. profound retardation.

3. Which of the following is not a communication disturbance found in autism?

   a. mutism
   b. reversal of "I" and "you"
   c. echolalia
   d. low tone speech

4. Research studies have shown that the emotional facial expressions, gestures, and vocalizations of an autistic child are often

   a. normal.
   b. flat.
   c. idiosyncratic.
   d. overly expressive.

5. Osterling and Dawson (1994) used a creative technique to diagnose autism. They

   a. reviewed snapshots of children.
   b. had the children tell a story with puppets.
   c. reviewed videotapes of first birthday parties.
   d. none of the above

6. What percentage of autistic children develop seizures after birth?

    a. 25
    b. 20
    c. 43
    d. 72

7. The genetics of autism suggest that

    a. autism is inherited directly.
    b. autism is not a genetic phenomenon.
    c. it is not inherited directly.
    d. it appears to skip a generation after transmission.

8. Through the use of scanning technology, researchers have discovered that autistic individuals appear to

    a. have a defective Y chromosome.
    b. have deficits in right hemisphere functioning.
    c. show stunted development in a part of the cerebellum.
    d. both b and c.

9. An intensive behavior modification program for autistic children which was developed by Lovaas indicated that

    a. autistic children respond poorly to the pressure generated by an intensive program.
    b. drug therapy was generally more successful than the behavior modification program.
    c. intensive behavioral training was superior to less intensive training and to the usual therapies used with autistic children.
    d. food was found to be ineffective as a reinforcer with these children.

10. A follow-up study of children diagnosed as autistic at a Canadian regional research center showed that

    a. most had more potential than formerly believed.
    b. most were living independently and holding jobs.
    c. most were living with parents who supervised their daily activities.
    d. most were in institutions and about 90% were mentally retarded.

11. Which of the following is true regarding autism versus mental retardation?

a. Self-stimulation is equally common among autistic and mentally retarded persons.
b. Autistic children are motivated to please adults but retarded children are not so motivated.
c. Retarded children show delays in language but autistic children show severe language deficits.
d. Self-stimulation is common in retardation but uncommon in autism.

12. Which of the statements below is not one of the diagnostic criteria for mental retardation?

a. The person has a significantly below-average level of intellectual functioning as measured by an IQ test.
b. The person has at least two out of eight standard physical characteristics that make a person appear retarded.
c. Social functioning is impaired.
d. It is an irreversible condition that begins before the age of 18.

13. The "first person" story of Temple Grandin, an autistic person, illustrates

a. a successful adjustment in life through development of an interest.
b. the shortened life span of the disorder.
c. that autistic individuals can also be psychotic.
d. the importance of behavior modification as a treatment for autism.

14. The majority of retarded people fall into the category of

a. mild retardation.
b. moderate retardation.
c. severe retardation.
d. savant retardation.

15. Mary is retarded but does not talk. She tends to respond to very simple commands and spends a great portion of her time rocking back and forth. Mary's retardation is probably in the _____ range.

a. severe
b. profound
c. mild
d. moderate

16. While it was formerly believed that mild mental retardation was due to a combination of heredity and environmental conditions, a Swedish study has shown that at least 50% of mentally retarded people have

   a. some chromosomal defect.
   b. a specific genetic disease.
   c. a pre- or postnatal disease.
   d. all of the above.

17. Disorders caused by predictable parental contributions are referred to as

   a. polygenic.
   b. innate.
   c. constitutional.
   d. recessive.

18. _____ is due to an abnormality of the sex chromosomes.

   a. Down syndrome
   b. Fragile X syndrome
   c. PKU
   d. Tay-Sachs disease

19. _____ occurs most often in people whose ancestors come from a small area in Eastern Europe.

   a. Tay-Sachs disease
   b. Fragile X syndrome
   c. PKU
   d. None of the above

20. Which is not a typical characteristic of children with Down syndrome?

   a. tallness
   b. flat face
   c. small nose
   d. congenital heart abnormality

21. Generally speaking, Down children seem especially weak in tactile perception, higher-level abstraction and reasoning, and

   a. socialization.
   b. perceptual-motor skills.
   c. facial discrimination.
   d. auditory perception.

22. Down syndrome children often learn better by

a. seeing material rather than hearing it.
b. hearing material rather than seeing it.
c. using verbal information rather than other methods of learning.
d. tactile perception rather than abstract reasoning.

23. Select the statement that is true of the average intellect of an adolescent or adult with Down syndrome.

a. They do not develop mentally beyond childhood.
b. Their cognitive abilities do not decrease with aging.
c. They are unemployable.
d. Stimulating environments may lead to intellectual development well into middle age.

24. _____ can not be successfully performed until the fourth month of pregnancy.

a. Chorionic villus sampling
b. Amniocentesis
c. The alpha-fetoprotein test
d. Spina bifida

25. Retardation may occur if a pregnant mother

a. contracts the rubella virus.
b. has syphilis.
c. has herpes.
d. all of the above.

26. Children born to mothers who drink heavily may

a. suffer retarded growth.
b. be born with physical deformities.
c. be born with mental retardation.
d. all of the above

27. Approximately _____ to_____ percent of variability in intelligence factors is due to genetics.

a. 50, 80
b. 10, 20
c. 80, 90
d. 20, 30

28. The results of studies focusing on psychosocial enrichment

    a. have demonstrated long-term effects.
    b. have not yet demonstrated long-term effects.
    c. are not concerned with long-term effects.
    d. show moderate but not long-term effects.

29. The 1975 Education for All Handicapped Children Act required

    a. parents to have children tested for mental retardation if a developmental delay was present before the age of five.
    b. public schools to provide free appropriate education to all handicapped children.
    c. required students to be "mainstreamed" at least for several hours during the school day.
    d. separate but equal learning facilities available for all handicapped children up to the age of 18 years.

30. The _____ often leads to a vulnerability for personal, sexual and financial exploitation.

    a. diminished cognitive abilities of retarded persons
    b. lack of social skills training in retarded persons
    c. use of group homes for the retarded
    d. tendency for retarded people to answer "yes"

31. An important part of a community-living program is

    a. the emphasis on contact with the family physician.
    b. the focus on job training.
    c. support offered by the federal government.
    d. the lack of supervision.

32. At present, theories of psychopathology among retarded persons

    a. lag behind those for the general population.
    b. are being intensively tested.
    c. are identical to those for the general population.
    d. point to commonalities between retarded persons and people from the general population.

TRUE/FALSE QUESTIONS

Indicate whether each statement is true or false. Check your answers at the end of this chapter.

1.   Autistic disorder is diagnosed on Axis II in DSM-IV.

2.   Approximately 75% of autistic cases involve some degree of mental retardation.

3.   Childhood schizophrenia usually occurs before age seven.

4.   Fifty percent of autistic children show a lack of symbolic play.

5.   According to research, there may be a hereditary factory in autism.

6.   Autistic children have difficulty generalizing learned responses.

7.   The genetics of autism suggest that a general tendency to have language or cognitive abnormalities is what is inherited from parents rather than autism.

8.   Mental retardation can be due to several factors.

9.   Many parents of retarded children retain some optimism about their child's future progress while the child is still young.

10.   The risk of giving birth to a child with Down syndrome increases dramatically with the age at which a woman becomes pregnant.

11.   Infants of adolescents are at high risk for retardation and other problems.

MATCHING

Match the following terms with information provided below. The answers may be found at the end of the chapter.

a.   PKU
b.   asphxia
c.   congenital factors
d.   fetal alcohol syndrome
e.   echolalia

f.   Trisomy 21
g.   moderate mental retardation
h.   mutants
i.   Fragile X syndrome

_____ includes innate plus prenatal conditions
_____ repeating what is heard

195

_____ lack of oxygen
_____ accounts for 10% of cases diagnosed as retarded
_____ another name for Down syndrome
_____ result of mother's heavy drinking while pregnant
_____ genes which are different from either parent
_____ abnormality of the sex chromosomes
_____ metabolic disorder for which newborns are screened

ANSWER KEY

Multiple Choice

1.d	17.b
2.c	18.b
3.d	19.a
4.c	20.a
5.c	21.d
6.b	22.a
7.c	23.d
8.c	24.b
9.c	25.d
10.d	26.d
11.c	27.a
12.b	28.b
13.a	29.b
14.a	30.d
15.b	31.b
16.d	32.a

True/False

1. F	7. T
2. T	8. T
3. F	9. T
4. T	10.T
5. T	11.T
6. T	

Matching

c
e
b
g
f
d
h
i
a

Chapter 17
THERAPIES AND THEIR OUTCOMES

CHAPTER OVERVIEW

The major approaches to treating maladaptive behavior are reviewed in the present chapter. The approaches considered are: psychodynamic, cognitive, behavioral, cognitive-behavioral, interpersonal therapy, and humanistic-existential. Prominent group therapies are also highlighted. The effectiveness of the various therapeutic styles is evaluated and methodological research issues considered. Finally, the scope and effectiveness of biological approaches are reviewed, and the changing role of the psychiatric hospital considered.

CHAPTER OUTLINE

Psychotherapy
>   Psychodynamic Therapy and Psychoanalysis
>   Humanistic and Existential Therapies
>   Cognitive Psychotherapy
>   Brief Psychotherapies
>   How Effective is Psychotherapy?

Cognitive-Behavioral Therapies
>   Behavior Therapy and Cognitive-Behavior Therapy
>   Components of Cognitive-Behavior Therapy

Group Therapy
>   Cognitive-Behavioral Group Therapy
>   Family and Marital Therapy
>   Psychodrama
>   How Effective are Group Approaches?

Research on the Psychological Therapies
>   Common and Unique Features of Therapies
>   Therapeutic Outcomes
>   Comparing Therapies
>   Cultural and Ethnic Diversity

Integration of Psychologically Based Therapeutic Approaches
Biological Therapies
>   Electroconvulsive Therapy
>   Drug Therapies

How Effective are Biological Therapies?

Hospitalization

LEARNING OBJECTIVES

You should know:

1.   how psychoanalysis and psychodynamic psychotherapy are structured and the concepts of free association, transference, and counter-transference.

2.   the goal of humanistic therapy, and the role and assumptions of the therapist in client-centered therapy.

3.   the assumptions and methods of the cognitive therapies including fixed-role, rational-emotive, and Beck's perspectives.

4.   the nature and techniques of Gestalt and existential therapies.

5.   the behavioral therapeutic paradigms including the specific types of techniques used to treat maladaptive behaviors.

6.   what group therapy is and how it is used to treat specific disorders.

7.   the methodological issues surrounding the study of therapeutic outcome and the contribution of meta-analysis to our understanding of therapeutic effectiveness.

8.   the commonalities among therapies and the inability to make a definitive statement regarding the most effective form of psychotherapy.

9.   the uses of electroconvulsive shock and drug therapies and the paradigms for evaluating their effectiveness.

10.   the changing role of the psychiatric hospital in the treatment of maladaptive behavior.

KEY TERMS AND CONCEPTS

Following is a list of key terms and concepts that are featured in the chapter and are important for you to know. Write out the definitions of each of these terms and check your answers with the definitions in the text.

psychodynamic therapy
psychoanalysis
free association
insight
transference
positive transference
negative transference
counter transference
hypnosis
humanistic therapies
client-centered therapy
unconditional positive regard
existential therapies
Gestalt therapy
cognitive psychotherapy
psychology of personal constructs
fixed-role therapy
rational-emotive therapy
interpersonal therapy
behavior modification
fading
token economy
biofeedback
cognitive-behavior therapy
relaxation training
exposure therapies
exposure
in vivo exposure
fantasized exposure
flooding
extinction
implosive therapy
systematic desensitization
paradoxical intention
modeling
guided rehearsals
live modeling
participant modeling
behavioral rehearsal

symbolic modeling
covert modeling
assertiveness training
family therapy
marital therapy
psychodrama
process research
spontaneous remission
meta-analysis
technique factors
interpersonal factors
electroconvulsive therapy
antipsychotic drugs
antimanic drugs
antidepressant drugs
antianxiety drugs
multimodal treatment
clinical trials
partial hospitalization
day hospital
deinstitutionalization

CRITICAL THINKING QUESTIONS

In developing answers for the following questions, turn to the section of your chapter that covers the pertinent material. Read the section thoroughly before attempting to frame your answer.

1. What are the characteristics common to all the various types of psychotherapy?

2. Describe the goals and procedures associated with traditional psychoanalysis.

3. What is the emphasis of humanistic therapy? Explain the client-centered approach of Carl Rogers.

4. Differentiate Gestalt therapy from existential therapy. What is interpersonal psychotherapy?

5. What are the assumptions and techniques associated with the cognitive psychotherapies?

6. Describe the techniques of behavior therapy.

7.   Explain the nature of cognitive-behavioral approaches. List and describe techniques used by this therapeutic model.

8.   Explain the concept of group therapy. What are some common features found among group therapies?

9.   What is family therapy? What types of problems does it attempt to address?

10.   How is marital therapy used?

11.   What are some of the methodological issues that must be considered in studies of psychotherapy effectiveness?

12.   How is therapy outcome measured?

13.   What does the research comparing effectiveness of therapeutic interventions tell us? What is meta-analysis?

14.   Distinguish technique factors from interpersonal factors as components of effective therapy? How may therapy research be improved?

15.   Describe the techniques used in biological therapies. Discuss the side-effects of medications used to treat maladaptive behavior.

16.   List the major reasons for hospitalization. What 10 steps does Paul (1969) recommend that hospitals take to increase effectiveness of the inpatient intervention? Is the role of the psychiatric hospital in treating disordered behavior changing?

MULTIPLE CHOICE

The following multiple choice questions will test your comprehension of the material presented in the chapter. Circle the correct choice for each question in the section, then compare your answers with those at the end of the chapter.

1.   Regardless of theoretical orientation, psychotherapists must perform three tasks. They must

    a. listen, understand, and advise.
    b. listen, understand, and respond.
    c. listen, advise, and evaluate.
    d. listen, interpret, and explore.

2. Psychoanalysis

   a. requires multiple weekly sessions.
   b. does not require that the patient develop insight into problems.
   c. has the client and therapist sitting face-to-face.
   d. is not suited to the use of free-association.

3. During a session of psychoanalysis a client begins to react emotionally toward the psychoanalyst as though the analyst were a parent. Treating the psychoanalyst as though he or she were an important figure from one's past is part of psychoanalysis called

   a. free association.
   b. developing insight.
   c. transference.
   d. countertransference.

4. Through interpretations, psychodynamically-oriented therapists

   a. attempt to expose areas of conflict.
   b. aid the client in gaining an understanding of past events.
   c. help the client put their motivation in perspective.
   d. all of the above.

5. A recent study by Williams (1994) on abuse victims found

   a. that the majority recalled false memories.
   b. that they actually did forget about the trauma.
   c. they had little insight into their situation.
   d. they tended to experience negative transference toward their therapist.

6. In 1994, a special committee of the American Psychological Association issued a report on memories of abuse. In the report, they state

   a. that it is not possible to repress memories of abuse.
   b. that there is no validation for the "false memory syndrome".
   c. that it is not possible to construct convincing pseudo-memories.
   d. that most people who were sexually abused remember part or all of what happened to them.

7. Which of the following statements is true regarding hypnosis?

   a. It is an acceptable treatment for severe mental disorders.
   b. It heightens a person's suggestibility.
   c. There are no harmful side effects.
   d. Dissociation and role-play do not appear to be associated with hypnosis.

8. Humanistic therapies emphasize the client's need

   a. to achieve insight.
   b. for achievement.
   c. for self-respect.
   d. to find the meaning of their existence.

9. Client-centered therapy is most associated with

   a. Kline.
   b. Rogers.
   c. Kelly.
   d. Frankel.

10. Perls, developer of Gestalt therapy, believed that the therapist's main task was to

    a. frustrate the client.
    b. provide unconditional positive regard.
    c. help the client understand the meaning of his/her own life.
    d. teach the client better methods of coping with problems.

11. According to cognitive therapists, unpleasant emotions such as depression and anger are caused by

    a. irrational beliefs.
    b. an inability to outwardly express emotions.
    c. early childhood traumas.
    d. a lack of unconditional positive regard.

12. In fixed-role therapy,

    a. clients try on new roles.
    b. clients come to accept their present roles as valid.
    c. clients have to tell the therapist what role he/she will play in therapy.
    d. both b & c.

13. During Rational-Emotive Therapy (RET) the client must

   a. develop insight into personal problems.
   b. identify, dispute, and replace irrational beliefs with rational ones.
   c. explore the therapeutic relationship and examine any transference.
   d. achieve self-respect.

14. "Automatic thoughts" are a concept employed by

   a. RET.
   b. fixed-role therapy.
   c. Beck's cognitive model.
   d. brief psychotherapies.

15. Interpersonal therapy

   a. focuses on interpersonal relationships.
   b. was originally designed to be used in the treatment of depression.
   c. assists the client in examining suppressed thoughts.
   d. all of the above.

16. Which of the factors below is a problem associated with evaluating the effectiveness of psychotherapy?

   a. therapists charge different patients different prices
   b. individual differences in therapists
   c. the personal biases of the researcher
   d. length of treatment

17. In a study by Najavits and Weiss (1994), therapeutic effectiveness was related to

   a. therapeutic orientation.
   b. the client's age.
   c. the length of treatment.
   d. the interpersonal skills of the therapist.

18. Which of the following is not a topic for process research?

   a. therapist/client perception of sessions
   b. therapist/client relationship
   c. treatment length
   d. content of therapeutic sessions

19. Select the therapist variable below that is not related to therapeutic change and outcome.

a. warmth
b. directness
c. beliefs
d. values

20. _____ is a method of quantifying therapeutic outcome measures so that they can be combined over several studies.

a. Meta-analysis
b. Factor analysis
c. Systematic analysis
d. Functional analysis

21. Which of the following is NOT a core characteristic of behavior therapy?

a. Clients must thoroughly explore early childhood experiences.
b. Most inappropriate behaviors can be modified through the application of social-learning principles.
c. Treatment methods are objectively evaluated.
d. Methods used during treatment are individually tailored to the differing needs of each client.

22. Which of the following is associated with behavior therapy?

a. insight
b. fading
c. positive reinforcement
d. both b & c

23. During therapy a phobic client learns to relax. Then while the client is relaxed, he or she imagines scenes that are related to the specific fear. The individual begins with imagining mildly upsetting scenes and gradually progresses to imagining highly upsetting scenes. This technique is known as

a. meditation.
b. autogenic training.
c. systematic desensitization.
d. in vivo exposure.

24. Sue's therapist asks her to hold a live snake because she reports having "snake phobia". The therapist is using

    a. fading.
    b. systematic desensitization.
    c. in vivo exposure.
    d. fantasy exposure.

25. Dylan tells his therapist that he is experiencing difficulty going to sleep at night. His therapist instructs him to remain awake at night as long as possible. The therapist is probably using a technique called

    a. modeling.
    b. paradoxical intention.
    c. implosion.
    d. aversion.

26. Select the factor below that influences the success of a modeling program.

    a. sex of the model
    b. observer's ability to copy model's behavior
    c. weight of the model
    d. observer's use of denial

27. Select the feature below that is not associated with group therapy.

    a. norm clarification
    b. self-containment
    c. social learning
    d. self-disclosure

28. Cognitive-behavioral group therapy would probably NOT emphasize

    a. graded task assignments.
    b. increasing social skills.
    c. analysis of transference.
    d. role playing.

29. A family therapist is likely to encourage the family to

    a. become more highly interdependent.
    b. work as a group to solve problems.
    c. become more closely knit and enmeshed.
    d. deal with problems in a more individual manner.

30.   In _____, a group of individuals assembles under the leadership of a therapist and enacts events of emotional significance in order to resolve conflicts.

a. family therapy
b. marital therapy
c. the systems approach
d. psychodrama

31.   Studies of improvement in psychotherapy should include which of the following?

a. the client's evaluation
b. the therapist's evaluation
c. the evaluation of family and friends
d. all of the above

32.   Discussions that center on the effectiveness of a particular type of therapy are expected to continue into the future because

a. not all persons who need treatment receive it.
b. therapists resist evaluation of therapeutic interventions.
c. all people benefit from some form of therapy.
d. there are no uniform criteria for assessing therapeutic effectiveness.

33.   In an effort to improve mental health services for members of minority groups, Paul Gordon suggests the relocation of mental health centers, employing therapists who share common backgrounds with clients, and

a. training of therapists.
b. decreasing fees.
c. providing on-site child care.
d. encouraging the client to become more Americanized.

34.   _____ drugs are used to treat bipolar disorders.

a. Antimanic
b. Antianxiety
c. Antipsychotic
d. Antidepressant

35.   Which of the following statements is FALSE about ECT?

a. Its use has increased in the past 20 years.
b. A major risk is memory loss.
c. Doctors don't know how ECT works.
d. There is a risk of spontaneous seizures.

TRUE/FALSE QUESTIONS

Indicate whether each statement is true or false. Check your answers at the end of this chapter.

1.   All forms of therapy are directed at finding out what is on the client's mind.

2.   Presently, there are a great number of psychodynamic approaches.

3.   Few psychologists today question the validity of repressed memories.

4.   The existential approach views the client as a "partner in treatment".

5.   Gestalt therapists do not believe that dreams are important sources of information about the client.

6.   Most cases of psychotherapy last fewer than 12 sessions.

7.   Eysenck concluded that psychotherapy was ineffective.

8.   Psychoanalysis is clearly more effective than other therapies.

9.   Cognitive therapy appears to be the treatment of choice for panic attacks.

10.   Relaxation therapy is not effective for psychosomatic disorders.

11.   Cognitive-behavioral treatments are effective for anxiety disorders.

12.   Families often have certain "myths".

13.   Less than 100 therapies are in use for adults according to Kazdin (1995).

14.   The average effectiveness rate for drugs used in treatment of maladaptive behavior is about 40%.

MATCHING

Match the following terms with information provided below. The answers may be found at the end of the chapter.

a. unconditional positive regard
b. spontaneous remission
c. covert modeling
d. free association
e. flooding

f. psychodrama
g. hypnosis
h. marital therapy
i. token economy
j. fixed role therapy

_____ a subtype of family therapy
_____ client practices new roles and relationships
_____ characterized by a natural flow of ideas
_____ uses operant principles to change behavior
_____ form of exposure therapy
_____ nonjudgmental stance of therapist
_____ client asked to imagine observing a model
_____ getting better without treatment
_____ acting out conflicts

ANSWER KEY

Multiple Choice

1. b
2. a
3. c
4. d
5. b
6. d
7. b
8. c
9. b
10. a
11. a
12. a
13. b
14. c
15. d
16. b
17. d
18. c

19. b
20. a
21. a
22. d
23. c
24. c
25. b
26. b
27. b
28. c
29. b
30. d
31. d
32. d
33. a
34. a
35. d

True/False

1. T	8. F
2. T	9. T
3. F	10. F
4. T	11. T
5. F	12. T
6. T	13. F
7. T	14. F

Matching

h
j
d
i
e
a
c
b
f

Chapter 18
SOCIETY'S RESPONSE TO MALADAPTIVE BEHAVIOR

CHAPTER OVERVIEW

This chapter concentrates on the issue of prevention and the role of the family, school and community in preventing and treating maladaptive behavior. Specific examples of existing programs for juvenile delinquency and suicide prevention are reviewed and the effectiveness of community programs evaluated. Legal aspects of treatment and prevention are explored and the use of paraprofessionals and self-help groups evaluated.

CHAPTER OUTLINE

Types of Prevention
      Levels of Prevention

Sites of Prevention
      The Family
      The School
      The Community

The Challenge of Prevention
      Paraprofessionals
      Self-help Groups
      Community Psychology

Treatment in the Community
      Problems with Community Programs
      Improving Treatment in the Community

Legal Aspects of Treatment and Prevention
      Institutionalization
      The Rights of Patients

A Final Word

LEARNING OBJECTIVES

You should know:

1. the difference between situation-focused and competency-based prevention.

2. the goals of primary, secondary, and tertiary prevention.

3. the impact of family variables such as child abuse, spouse abuse, and divorce on the development of abnormal behavior. It is also important to know prevention efforts that might limit the impact of these variables.

4. the goals of early education and screening programs in the educational process.

5. the types of community programs that can facilitate living in the community as opposed to residing in institutions, and the effectiveness of deinstitutionalization.

6. the requirements for criminal commitment.

7. the rulings derived from the M'Naghten Rule and the American Law Institute guidelines.

8. the two judgements that must be made before a civil commitment can be ordered.

9. what paraprofessionals are and their role in mental health programs.

10. the major characteristics of self-help groups and how they operate to benefit their members.

KEY TERMS AND CONCEPTS

Following is a list of key terms and concepts that are featured in the chapter and are important for you to know. Write out the definitions of each of these terms and check your answers with the definitions in the text.

situation-focused prevention
competency-focused prevention
primary prevention
secondary prevention
tertiary prevention
juvenile delinquency
child abuse
spouse abuse

postvention
commitment
criminal commitment
civil commitment
irresistible impulse
Durham Rule
informed consent
insanity
competency
incompetent person
M'Naghten rule
parens patriae
custodial housing
alternative housing
paraprofessional
self-help groups
community psychology

CRITICAL THINKING QUESTIONS

In developing answers for the following questions, turn to the section of your chapter that covers the pertinent material. Read each section thoroughly before attempting to frame your answer.

1. What is the difference between situation and competency-focused prevention? Give examples of each.

2. What are the goals of primary, secondary, and tertiary prevention?

3. Define juvenile delinquency and list conditions associated with this phenomenon.

4. Explain the concept of child abuse. What are the characteristics of abusing families? What interventions are used to prevent child abuse?

5. What is spouse abuse? List the different self-statements used to treat victims of this abuse.

6. How does divorce impact children? Describe the role of parents as therapists.

7. What role can the school play in primary prevention of disordered behavior?

8. How can the community assist in prevention efforts?

9. List the warning signs of suicide. Describe the suicide postvention process.

10. Explain the issues involving treatment in the community.

11. Differentiate between civil and criminal commitment. How are competency and insanity defined? What is the M'Naghten rule?

12. Do patients have rights? Explain the concept of "informed consent".

13. How has the use of paraprofessionals and self-help groups contributed to prevention efforts?

MULTIPLE CHOICE

The following multiple choice questions will test your comprehension of the material presented in the chapter. Circle the correct choice for each question in the section, then compare your answers with those at the end of the chapter.

1. The reduction or elimination of the environmental causes of distressed behavior is an example of

   a. tertiary prevention.
   b. situation-focused prevention.
   c. competency-focused prevention.
   d. community intervention.

2. Which of the following would be an example of primary prevention?

   a. premarital counseling
   b. marital therapy
   c. behavior therapy for a hyperactive child
   d. post-rape supportive group counseling

3. Prenatal classes for parents-to-be, which focus on the importance of an appropriate diet and provide information about the effects of smoking and drinking during pregnancy, would be a type of

   a. primary prevention.
   b. secondary prevention.
   c. tertiary prevention.
   d. behavioral intervention.

4.   Tertiary prevention is aimed at reducing

       a. the number of new cases of a disorder in a given population.
       b. the duration of an existing abnormal condition.
       c. the intensity of an existing disorder.
       d. the impairment that may result from a disorder or event.

5.   Which of the following conditions has been associated with an increased risk of
       delinquency?

       a. parental support for academic achievement
       b. alcoholic parents
       c. birth order
       d. none of the above

6.   Which of the following is NOT one of the typical characteristics of an abusive
       parent compared to a non-abusive parent?

       a. lower level of intelligence
       b. less self-critical
       c. more aggressive
       d. more tense

7.   Parents can be taught to respond therapeutically to their children's behavioral
       problems mainly through the techniques of

       a. play therapy and sharing feelings.
       b. modeling, behavioral rehearsal, and reinforcement.
       c. unconditional positive regard and listening.
       d. sharing their negative feelings with children and allowing them to know what
       problems the adult is experiencing.

8.   _____ % of the women murdered in the U.S. were killed by a husband, ex-husband
       or suitor.

       a. Fifty-one
       b. Twenty-nine
       c. Three
       d. None of the above

9. Which of the following characteristics is not typical of a wife abuser?

   a. tension
   b. resentment
   c. suspicion
   d. narcicism

10. Select the characteristic that is typical of a boy's reaction to familial conflict.

    a. troubled peer relations
    b. poor school grades
    c. overidentification with the father
    d. rejection of peers

11. If a therapist is trying to advise parents on how to soften the blow of divorce, she might suggest

    a. not telling the children ahead of time.
    b. explaining the reasons for the divorce.
    c. setting strong limits on the child's anger.
    d. reinforcing the notion that things will pretty much continue on as before.

12. After a year of participation in the cognitive and social skills program designed by Sarason and Sarason, participating high school students

    a. were rated as being more popular by peers than a control group.
    b. had better school attendance and less tardiness than the control group.
    c. were more likely to find after-school jobs than the control group.
    d. had higher grade point averages than the control group.

13. The study by Ross and Glaser of male residents in a large city ghetto found that higher success in work situations is related to

    a. approval from peers.
    b. more independence from family.
    c. early diet and nutrition.
    d. encouragement and discipline at home.

14. When a friend or family member seems to be suicidal, it would probably NOT be a good idea to

    a. ask them, "Are you thinking of killing yourself?"
    b. ignore them.
    c. contact a suicide prevention center.
    d. ask them, "Are you unhappy?"

15. Find the factor below that is not a warning sign of suicide.

   a. giving away possessions
   b. withdrawal from friends
   c. ending a love relationship
   d. moving to a new apartment

16. Paraprofessionals

   a. have not been found to be effective in community mental health centers.
   b. tend to vary in age, education and cultural background.
   c. are labor-intensive to train.
   d. none of the above.

17. Self-help groups benefit their members through

   a. providing models on how to cope effectively with stress.
   b. encouraging catharsis.
   c. providing a social outlet.
   d. allowing the participant to accurately lay blame.

18. Community psychology is

   a. a subdiscipline of clinical psychology.
   b. concerned with the role of social systems in preventing maladaptive behavior.
   c. currently undergoing a dramatic revision.
   d. both a & b.

19. In community psychology, alternative housing refers to

   a. half-way houses.
   b. nursing homes.
   c. special-care homes.
   d. custodial housing.

20. The Oxford House concept

   a. has not been effective in reducing rehospitalization.
   b. is fully supported by federal funding.
   c. is synonymous with self-governance.
   d. points to the need for dramatic reform of the half-way house concept.

21. The case of Sylvia Frumkin has led to

    a. a focus on system and legal reforms.
    b. increased use of lithium in the elderly.
    c. a recognition of schizophrenia as a genetic problem.
    d. both b and c.

22. Which of the following is required by the chronically mentally ill living in the community?

    a. support for family members
    b. clinical services
    c. adequate, supervised housing
    d. all of the above

23. Civil commitment involves whether the individual

    a. is capable of holding a job.
    b. has had a history of violent behavior in the past.
    c. is sane or insane.
    d. is a risk to himself or herself, or to others.

24. _____ refers to a person's state of mind at the time of a judicial proceeding.

    a. Competency
    b. Schizophrenia
    c. Insanity
    d. Illness

25. The M'Naghten rule is most closely associated with

    a. crimes committed by normal people.
    b. a knowledge of right or wrong.
    c. John Hinckley's plea of sanity.
    d. none of the above.

26. "Irresistible impulse" means

    a. the individual's behavior was not necessarily illegal.
    b. the individual could not discriminate right from wrong.
    c. the individual could not control his behavior.
    d. both b & c.

27. "Parens patriae" is a Latin term which means

   a. parenthood to the state.
   b. parents should be parents.
   c. parenting makes patriots.
   d. parenthood is achieved through patience.

28. According to Appelbaum (1991), a mental health practitioner's success rate for predicting near future dangerous behavior is between

   a. 80-90%.
   b. 50-70%.
   c. 40-60%.
   d. 20-40%.

29. Informed consent requires

   a. that patients receive adequate information about planned treatment before they agree to submit to it.
   b. that patients tell their therapists relevant background information prior to the onset of treatment.
   c. that both patient and therapist agree through a contract on treatment goals.
   d. that a patient have a "sanity hearing" within 7 days of entering an institution under commitment.

30. In the formula P=KxW, the P, K, and W stand for

   a. prevention, knowledge, and will.
   b. personality, knowledge, and work.
   c. professionals, knowledge, and willingness to help.
   d. personal effectiveness, kindness, and willingness to help.

TRUE/FALSE

Indicate whether each statement is true or false. Check your answers at the end of this chapter.

1. Between 4% and 5% of American teens are referred to courts annually.

2. The adolescent pregnancy rate is approximately 500,000 cases per year.

3. There appears to be a strong link between alcoholic parents and hyperactive offspring.

4. Thirty percent of all women with a spouse or living with a partner have been beaten at least once in the relationship.

5. Divorce and familial conflict appear to affect the development of children.

6. Unemployment appears to be stressful only to those of lower economic status.

7. Most people who commit suicide are psychologically disturbed.

8. One way to prevent suicide is to restrict access of high-risk individuals to drugs that are lethal in high doses.

9. Many conversations we have daily may be viewed as mutual counseling sessions.

10. One hundred thousand mentally ill individuals are confined to prison every day.

MATCHING

Match the following terms with information provided below. The answers may be found at the end of the chapter.

a.	paraprofessional	f.	spouse abuse
b.	competency	g.	self-help groups
c.	P=KxW	h.	postvention program
d.	Rennie v. Klein	i.	criminal commitment
e.	community psychology	j.	informed consent

_____ 25 to 30% of all women living with a partner have been beaten at least once while in this relationship
_____ applies to patients and experimental subjects
_____ allowed patients to refuse treatment
_____ may fill gap between professionals and lower socioeconomic groups
_____ involves placing someone who has broken the law into a mental hospital
_____ members share common concerns
_____ concerned with role of social systems in preventing human distress
_____ prevention formula
_____ designed to help people who knew someone who committed suicide

ANSWER KEY

Multiple Choice

1.b	16.b
2.a	17.a
3.a	18.b
4.d	19.a
5.b	20.c
6.b	21.a
7.b	22.d
8.b	23.d
9.d	24.a
10.a	25.b
11.b	26.c
12.b	27.a
13.d	28.c
14.b	29.a
15.d	30.a

True/False

1. T	6. F
2. F	7. T
3. T	8. T
4. T	9. T
5. T	10. F

Matching

f
j
d
a
i
g
e
c
h